# PRACTICE TESTS FOR CAMBRIDGE CERTIFICATE OF
# PROFICIENCY
## IN ENGLISH

**NEW SYLLABUS**

D1731405

## TEACHER'S EDITION
### SET TWO

MARGARET ARCHER  ENID NOLAN-WOODS

Nelson

Thomas Nelson and Sons Ltd
Nelson House   Mayfield Road
Walton-on-Thames   Surrey
KT12 5PL   UK

51 York Place
Edinburgh
EH1 3JD   UK

Thomas Nelson (Hong Kong) Ltd
Toppan Building 10/F
22A Westlands Road
Quarry Bay   Hong Kong

Distributed in Australia by

Thomas Nelson Australia
480 La Trobe Street
Melbourne   Victoria 3000
and in Sydney, Brisbane, Adelaide and Perth

© Margaret Archer and Enid Nolan-Woods 1986

First published by Thomas Nelson and Sons Ltd 1986

Reprinted in 1987

ISBN 0-17-555654-7

NCN 71-ECE-9244-02

Printed in Great Britain by Ebenezer Baylis and Son Ltd, Worcester

## ACKNOWLEDGEMENTS

The publishers are grateful to the following for permission to reproduce
copyright material. They have tried to contact all copyright holders, but in cases where they may have failed will be pleased to make the necessary arrangements at the first opportunity.

University of Cambridge Local Examinations Syndicate for the specimen answer sheet; William Heinemann Ltd for an extract from *Delight* by J B Priestley; Punch for three extracts from the *Punch Book of Travel*; Mark Ottaway for the passage from his article *Know Your Place* printed in the *Sunday Times* magazine (5.1.86); Faber and Faber for an extract from *Required Writing* by Philip Larkin; *The Times* for the article *Boost for Backers of Renewable Energy* by Pearce Wright (4.5.84) J M Dent and Sons Ltd for an extract from *Trumps* by Frankie Howerd; A D Peters and Co Ltd for an extract from the introduction to *A Book of Railway Journeys* by Ludovic Kennedy; London Borough of Camden for their information leaflet on Sheltered Housing; *Daily Telegraph* for the article *Setting Designs on the Fashion Business* by Edward Fennell (30.1.84); Oxford University Press for an extract from the editorial of *ELT Journal* Volume 40/3 July 1986 published in association with The British Council; London Regional Transport for the leaflet See all the Sights with Us; *The Observer* for an article by Sue Baker entitled *Reserved for Nature* (19.1.86); Patrick Marnham for an extract from his book *So Far From God*; The Electricity Council for part of the leaflet *Safety in Your Home*; Routledge and Kegan Paul for an extract from *Reading from Process to Practice*; *The Sunday Times* for the article *Time to Lower the Gangway* (27.5.84) by Richard Brooks; International Association of Teachers of English as a Foreign Language for their information sheet on Examinations for Students of English; *Life in the Future* by Malcolm Ross-Macdonald et al, copyright 1976, Aldus Books Limited by permission of the copyright owner.

Copyright photographs are reproduced by courtesy of the following:
Kobal collection p.17; Ralph Steadman p.18; Sally and Richard Greenhill pp.36, 60, 78 and 99; Rex Features pp. 59 and 61; Tate Gallery p.100; Nouvelles Images editeurs and Ronald Searle p.100; Victoria and Albert Museum (Crown) p.101

Cover photograph from *The Talented Mr Ripley* (Penguin Books) reproduced by kind permission of Penguin Books.

Cover photograph of *The Entertainer* by courtesy of International Creative Management Ltd.

# Contents

**Notes to the Teacher**
Examination Format
Marking Scheme

# Notes to the Teacher

## EXAMINATION FORMAT

The object of this book is to provide students preparing for the Cambridge Certificate of Proficiency in English with complete practice in the Written and Oral papers. Each of the five tests consists of three written and two oral papers as follows:

### WRITTEN PAPERS

**Paper 1 Reading Comprehension** (1 hour)

Section A Twenty-five multiple choice questions testing vocabulary and formal grammatical control, in sentence contexts.

Section B Fifteen multiple choice reading comprehension questions based on three or more texts, designed to test gist, detailed content, recognition of form, register and intention, etc.

**Paper 2 Composition** (2 hours)

Two compositions from a choice of descriptive, situational or discursive topics, or topics based on prescribed reading. Assessment will be based on organisation and clarity of content, accuracy of grammatical control, fluency and range of expression.

**Paper 3 Use of English** (2 hours)

Section A Open-completion or transformation items designed to test active control of the patterns and usage of English.

Section B Questions on a passage designed to test ability to understand, interpret and summarise.

### ORAL PAPERS

**Paper 4 Listening Comprehension** (Approx. 30 minutes)

Questions of varying type (selection, re-ordering, blank-filling, etc.) to test accurate understanding of spoken English, based on recorded material including conversation, announcements, etc.

**Paper 5 Interview** (Approx. 15 minutes)

Based on a picture stimulus, and thematically-related passages and other material. The interview may, optionally, be based partly on one of the prescribed texts. It may be conducted, also optionally, with individual candidates or in groups of two or three. Assessment will be based on fluency and grammatical accuracy, pronunciation, communicative ability and vocabulary. Candidates will not be required to read aloud.

Cassettes of the Listening Comprehension material for Paper 4 are available.

# MARKING SCHEME

Certificates are awarded in three grades A, B and C on the aggregate of marks gained in the five papers, with results also in two failing grades D and E.

## Paper 1    Reading Comprehension

An incorrect answer gains no mark, but no marks are specifically deducted for wrong answers.

Section A    25 items—1 mark each        25
Section B    15 items—2 marks each       30

Final mark weighting for Paper 1        **40 marks**

## Paper 2    Composition

2 compositions—20 marks each

The following are guidelines for assessment:

| 18—20 | Excellent | Error-free, substantial and varied material, resourceful and controlled in language and expression. |
| 16—17 | Very Good | Good realisation of task, ambitious and natural in style. |
| 12—15 | Good | Sufficient assurance and freedom from basic error to maintain theme. |
| 8—11 | Pass | Clear realisation of task, reasonably correct and natural. |
| 5—7 | Weak | Near to pass level in general scope, but with either numerous errors or too elementary or translated in style. |
| 0—4 | Very Poor | Basic errors, narrowness of vocabulary. |

Final mark weighting for Paper 2        **40 marks**

## Paper 3    Use of English

An average 15 marks are allotted per question, but the working total of marks for the paper is kept variable to give better discrimination and coverage of the expected 'syllabus' of functions, structures, etc. for the paper. Section B carries about 20% of the total mark. The final question, in Section B, is a test of ability to interpret and summarise, and marks are given for coherent and relevant answers.

Final mark weighting for Paper 3        **40 marks**

## Paper 4    Listening Comprehension

The final total may involve adjustments of scores on a larger number of individual items than the marks allotted, to give control over the desirable weighting of answers for discriminating purposes, and to offset, for instance, the guessing factor in true/false selection items.

Final mark weighting for Paper 4        **20 marks**

**Paper 5   Interview**

The marking of the interview will be by impression, using detailed marking grades. The examiners' assessments are made on six scales continuously throughout the interview, as follows:

**Fluency**   Speed and rhythm, choice of structures, general naturalness and clarity.
**Grammatical accuracy**   Control of structures including tenses, prepositions, etc. to an effective level of communication.
**Pronunciation (Sentences)**   Stress, timing and intonation patterns linking of phrases.
**Pronunciation (Individual sounds)**   Differentiation of consonants and vowels in stressed and unstressed position. Natural timbre and basis of articulation.
**Interactive communication**   Flexibility and linguistic resource in exchange of information and social interaction.
**Vocabulary resource**   Variety and correctness of vocabulary in the communicative context.

Examples of grading specifications as used by examiners are as follows:
(Interactive Communication)

| 5 | Wholly effective at communicating in all contexts. |
|---|---|
| 4 | Communicates effectively and with ease in most contexts, experiencing only occasional difficulty. |
| 3 | Communicates effectively and with ease in everyday contexts and adequately in more abstract contexts. Does not try the listener's patience. |
| 2 | Communication effective in everyday contexts but demands excessive patience in more abstract contexts. |
| 1 | Communicates poorly even in everyday contexts. |
| 0 | Communicates nothing. |

(Pronunciation: Sentences)

| 5 | Virtually native-speaker stress-timing, rhythm and placing of stress, intonation patterns and range of pitch within sentence, natural linking of phrases. |
|---|---|
| 4 | Stress-timing, rhythm, placing of stress, intonation, etc. sufficiently native-like as to make comprehension easy and listening pleasurable. |
| 3 | Stress-timing, rhythm, placing of stress, intonation, etc. sufficiently controlled. |
| 2 | Foreign speech patterns make the candidate occasionally difficult to understand. |
| 1 | Foreign speech patterns severely impede comprehension. |
| 0 | Not intelligible, through faulty stress and intonation. |

The framework for the Interview, which lasts 12–15 minutes, takes a number of forms, using a combination of visual stimuli and verbal prompting from the examiner, and moving from simple identification of material (with due care taken not to test factual knowledge or ability to absorb detailed information) to discussion of associated topics. Candidates may choose to take the interview on their own or with one or two other candidates. Where the group option is chosen, candidates may be given the same material to discuss or each candidate may be given a different photograph, passage, leaflet and so on and asked to explain it or describe it to the other candidates. Examiners may supplement the material provided with their own photographs or passages, etc. on the same topic.

Final mark weighting for Paper 5      **40 marks**

**Total for the whole examination**      **180 marks**

# CAMBRIDGE CERTIFICATE OF PROFICIENCY IN ENGLISH

## TESTS 1–5

# Test One

*Answer all questions. Indicate your choice of answer in every case* **on the separate answer sheet** *already given out, which should show your name and examination index number. Follow carefully the instructions about how to record your answers. Give* **one answer only** *to each question. Marks will not be deducted for wrong answers: your total score on this test will be the number of correct answers you give.*

### SECTION A

*In this section you must choose the word or phrase which best completes each sentence.* **On your answer sheet** *indicate the letter A, B, C or D against the number of each item 1 to 25 for the word or phrase you choose.*

1   Computer games ............... me, they are so confusing.
    A ruffle      B snaffle      C baffle      D scuttle

2   ............... he was found guilty, he was only put on probation.
    A However      B Despite      C Therefore      D Although

3   There will be a meeting of the ............... of Directors tomorrow afternoon.
    A Board      B Committee      C Council      D Cabinet

4   I know you think she's weak-willed but I've always found her very ............... .
    A quick-witted      B strong-minded      C self-centred      D hard-hearted

5   He used so much jargon that I hadn't a ............... what he was talking about.
    A query      B hint      C thought      D clue

6   Isn't it time you ............... some serious work before the examination?
    A got down to      B took up with      C got off with      D put down to

7   The ............... of employment are set out in the contract.
    A arrangements      B conditions      C requirements      D specifications

8   We are making an ............... effort to increase production.
    A all in      B altogether      C all out      D all together

9   The whole story was a ............... of his imagination.
    A figure      B figment      C fantasy      D fabrication

10   Did you get any ............... effects when you were taking those tablets?
    A subsidiary      B backwash      C subsequent      D side

11  The water was ............... by waste from the factory.
    A contaminated    B infected    C putrified    D infested

12  Williams was taken off the short list for the job as his appointment would have caused
    a lot of ............... .
    A challenge    B controversy    C dilemma    D dissidence

13  After the interval, the change of ............... brought a gasp of surprise from the
    audience.
    A scene    B vista    C panorama    D view

14  It was hoped that the Government would ............... abolishing the Metropolitan
    Councils.
    A run away from    B stand back from    C let go of    D think better of

15  I must remember to ............... my TV licence next month.
    A regain    B replace    C renew    D retain

16  He made a very ............... excuse for not attending the meeting.
    A faint    B feeble    C frail    D fragile

17  According to the retail price ............... inflation is down by 2%.
    A index    B bulletin    C list    D report

18  The most common ............... for murder is money.
    A cause    B motive    C source    D factor

19  He decided to go to London on the ............... of the moment.
    A reflex    B hunch    C spur    D idea

20  I should like to ............... your attention to the new parking regulations.
    A pay    B give    C draw    D focus

21  Glancing ............... his shoulder, he noticed he was being followed.
    A back    B round    C behind    D over

22  We're interrupting this programme for a news ............... .
    A flash    B signal    C alarm    D alert

23  As a result of increased productivity, the workers received a ............... pay increase.
    A palpable    B substantial    C fundamental    D tangible

24  The plastic ............... of my glasses is easily broken.
    A support    B holder    C frame    D surround

25  The going ............... for the job is £5 an hour.
    A pay    B wage    C price    D rate

## SECTION B

*In this section you will find after each of the passages a number of questions or unfinished statements about the passage, each with four suggested answers or ways of finishing. You must choose the one you think fits best according to the passage.* **On your answer sheet** *indicate the letter A, B, C or D against the number of each item 26 to 40 for the answer you choose. Give* **one answer only** *to each question. Read each passage right through before choosing your answers.*

## FIRST PASSAGE

Quietly malicious chairmanship. There is no sound excuse for this. It is deeply antisocial, and a sudden excess of it would tear great holes in our communal life. But a man can be asked once too often to act as chairman, and to such a man, despairing of his weakness and feeling a thousand miles from any delight, I can suggest a few devices. In introducing one or two of the chief speakers, grossly over-praise them but put no warmth in your voice, only a metallic flavour of irony. If you know what a speaker's main point is to be, then make it neatly in presenting him to the audience. During some tremendous peroration which the chap has been working on for days, either begin whispering and passing notes to other speakers or give the appearance of falling asleep in spite of much effort to keep awake. If the funny man takes possession of the meeting and brings out the old jokes, either look melancholy or raise your eyebrows as high as they will go. Announce the fellow with the weak delivery in your loudest and clearest tones. For any timid speaker, officiously clear a space bang in the middle and offer him water, paper, pencil, a watch, anything. With noisy, cheeky chaps on their feet, bustle about the platform, and if necessary give a mysterious little note to some member of the audience. If a man insists upon speaking from the floor of the hall, ask him for his name, pretend to be rather deaf, and then finally, announce his name with a marked air of surprise. After that you can have some trouble with a cigarette lighter and then take it to pieces. When they all go on and on, make no further pretence of paying any attention and settle down to drawing outrageous caricatures of the others on the platform, and then at last ask some man you particularly dislike to take over the chair, and stalk out, being careful to leave all your papers behind. And if all this fails to bring you any delight, it should at least help to protect you against further bouts of chairmanship.

26  The advice in this passage is intended to help chairmen to
   A   be less boring.
   B   cut short a meeting.
   C   enliven a dull meeting.
   D   gain useful experience.

27  A chairman can distract a lengthy speaker by making a show of
   A   shuffling papers.
   B   nodding off.
   C   passing him a note.
   D   muttering to himself.

28   If a speaker is nervous, the writer suggests that the chairman should
    A   do everything to assist him.
    B   confuse him with unnecessary help.
    C   offer to take notes for him.
    D   clear the platform for him.

29   When a speaker shows no sign of stopping, the chairman should
    A   ask him to take the chair.
    B   draw a flattering picture of him.
    C   pretend not to be paying attention.
    D   leave ostentatiously.

30   The tone of this passage is
    A   spiteful.
    B   humorous.
    C   sarcastic.
    D   mischievous.

## SECOND PASSAGE

Americans are people obsessed with child-rearing. In their books, magazines, talk shows, parent training courses, White House conferences, and chats over the back fence, they endlessly debate the best ways to raise children. Moreover, Americans do more than debate their theories; they translate them into action. They erect playgrounds for the youngsters' pleasure, equip large schools for their education, and train skilled specialists for their welfare. Whole industries in America are devoted to making children happy, healthy and wise.

But this interest in childhood is relatively new. In fact, until very recently people considered childhood just a brief, unimportant prelude to adulthood and the real business of living. By and large they either ignored children, beat them, or fondled them carelessly, much as we would amuse ourselves with a litter of puppies. When they gave serious thought to children at all, people either conceived of them as miniature adults or as peculiar, unformed animals.

Down through the ages the experiences of childhood have been as varied as its duration. Actions that would have provoked a beating in one era elicit extra loving care in another. Babies who have been nurtured exclusively by their mothers in one epoch are left with day-care workers in another. In some places children have been trained to straddle unsteady canoes, negotiate treacherous mountain passes, and carry heavy bundles on their heads. In other places they have been taught complicated piano concerti and long multiplication tables.

But diverse as it has been, childhood has one common experience at its core and that is the social aspect of nurture. All children need adults to bring them up. Because human young take so long to become independent, we think that civilization may have grown up around the need to feed and protect them. Certainly, from the earliest days of man, adults have made provision for the children in their midst.

31  The present day American obsession with child-rearing has
   A  resulted in ineffectual action.
   B  initiated pointless discussions.
   C  had wide-ranging results.
   D  produced endless theories.

32  Children in the past were ill-treated or petted because they were
   A  ignorant of adult life.
   B  seen as uninteresting.
   C  considered of no importance.
   D  conceived of as having animal natures.

33  How have childhood experiences varied?
   A  Children have been alternately beaten and loved through the ages.
   B  There have been differences in child-rearing in different epochs.
   C  Parents have increasingly taken control of their children's nurturing.
   D  In some places physical training has given way to encouraging creativity.

34  According to the author, children
   A  need intensive adult nurturing.
   B  are the instigators of civilization.
   C  remain physically dependent until adulthood.
   D  have common social experiences.

35  What is the author's attitude to developments in the perception of childhood?
   A  Cynical.
   B  Indifferent.
   C  Positive.
   D  Neutral.

## THIRD PASSAGE

*A*

My dream is to turn up at Heathrow. . . Commissionaires in white gloves would park my car for me, and a senior official would take my ticket and passport away for processing and I would be hurried to a small room away from the hurly-burly and be persuaded to accept eight or nine glasses of Dom Perignon. A small car would take me out to the aircraft. At the top of the ladder I would be welcomed aboard by the chief stewardess, a recent Miss World . . . Drawing myself up to my full height in order to acknowledge her greeting I would then crash my head into the top of the metal doorway and drop, senseless, at her feet. I would recover consciousness just as the aircraft drew to a halt at our destination, the stewardess forcing five-star Duty-Free between my wan lips; all flying flown.

*B*

In a walled city, too small to need cars, full of attractive, happy, prosperous citizens in a permanent state of fiesta. A language you don't feel ashamed not to speak, but like English with a comic accent you can learn in a day. A hotel with a room on stilts out in the bay. No papers but all news transmitted by gossip over drinks. Drinks like childhood lemonade, but non-fattening, and alcoholic without hangovers. Food like fish and chips, but non-dyspeptic and in every possible flavour. Ancient remains, only half-excavated, where you can find a gold necklace by digging with your big toe. A volcano which erupts only at midnight pouring a ration of lava safely out to sea. Weather warm, but not too sunny or sunny, but not too scorching. I don't know who arranges such holidays. If I did, I wouldn't tell you.

*C*

I want to go to South America and see Rio, I'd love to tour the West Indies, I've got the feeling that if I went to Hawaii I might never come back. The thought of visiting Japan fascinates me and Ceylon is an exotic mystery I would love to investigate. I have not been to any of these places and I would like to do so. And what about the places I've been to and want to revisit. I'd like once more to see the sun set on Jerusalem, April in Paris, autumn in New York, any time in San Francisco and Dublin when it's raining and I feel like getting drunk and listening to good talk. So my perfect trip would be a discovery of new wonders and also old joys revisited.

*D*

One day I got off a ferry in a Greek village and found after a few days I had fallen amongst friends. I discovered that, instead of wanting to move on as usual, the more I knew about the village and its people the more I wanted to know, and the richer each discovery became.

The village is called Lakka, on Paxos. . . The essence of Lakka is that it has no sandy beaches (but crystal waters) and no hotels. Tourists stay in rooms or houses that, for the most part, belong to the local people who thus directly benefit from our stay while restaurants compete amiably for our custom. . . There is no 'entertainment', just peace, quiet and the smiles of people who take a long-term view of your happiness and theirs, and want nothing more than for you to come back next year. It is tourism at its best.

36   Which extract, A, B, C or D, conveys the impression that the writer is gregarious?

37   In which extract, A, B, C, or D, does the writer refer to VIP treatment?

38   Which extract, A, B, C, or D, conveys an air of tranquillity?

39   One of the extracts suggests the writer is adventurous. Which one? A, B, C or D.

40   Which extract, A, B, C or D, suggests the writer has a conservative nature?

# PAPER 2 COMPOSITION (2 hours)

*Write **two only** of the following composition exercises. Your answers must follow exactly the instructions given. Write in pen, not pencil. You are allowed to make alterations, but see that your work is clear and easy to read.*

1 Describe a state ceremony in your country, giving reasons why it is held. (About 350 words)

2 'Everyone has the right to work.' Discuss. (About 350 words)

3 Write a story that begins as follows: 'It seemed a day much the same as any other until. . .' (About 350 words)

4 Using the information in the following notes, write out an announcement to the staff of a department store warning them of an increase in shop-lifting and thefts of staff property and telling them what action to take. (About 350 words)

> ### *Theft of Staff Property*
>
> Property to be kept under lock and key
> Store takes no responsibility for property left unlocked
>
> ### *Shop-lifting*
>
> *Keep careful watch for:*
> customers with large carrier bags
> goods being examined at length
> loiterers at crowded counters
> unaccompanied children
> customers wearing unusually loose clothing
>
> *Be alert for:*
> price tags being removed from goods on display
> customers leaving in undue haste
> the removal of goods from packaging

5 (See Appendix: Prescribed texts)

# PAPER 3  USE OF ENGLISH  (2 hours)

*Answer **all** the questions.*
*Your answers must be written in ink in this booklet, using the spaces provided.*

## SECTION A

1  *Fill each of the numbered blanks in the following passage with **one** suitable word.*

The domestic cat has a wild life. Cats are enigmatic and tough. Dainty in the discipline of ............................ (1) daily grooming, they are dirty in a fight – they claw at ............................ (2) another's scruples. Cats move beautifully and ............................ (3) inscrutably. They are survivors. Cats inspire in ............................ (4) reverence and love or fear and dislike but, above all ............................ (5), they inspire curiosity.

............................ (6) cats play games? We know ............................ (7) they practise the ............................ (8) of mice, the capture of birds, and the theft, ............................ (9) possible, of our ............................ (10) supermarket-acquired carrion. But all ............................ (11) is their trade, their work.

Yet, we fondly ............................ (12) cats ............................ (13) shadow games, lifting ping-pong ............................ (14), nudging pens and pencils ............................ (15) tables, and ............................ (16) at door handles. On the one ............................ (17), we know that with ............................ (18) pranks they ............................ (19) their killing craft, but we suspect they also enjoy ............................ (20) – just as we enjoy their games.

2  *Finish each of the following sentences in such a way that it means exactly the same as the sentence printed before it.*

    EXAMPLE:  She didn't turn the TV off.

    ANSWER:  The TV *was left switched on.* ............................

  a)  He has a strong objection to travelling by train.
     He absolutely ................................................................................................

  b)  Can we hire a car from the airport?
     Is it ..................................................................................................................... ?

  c)  I didn't quite catch your name.
     Would you ..................................................................................................... ?

d) 'Don't go too far out – the sea's very rough,' Peter told his girlfriend.
Peter warned ......................................................................................................

e) You can't buy stamps at the supermarket.
The supermarket ................................................................................................

f) Hurry up or you won't catch the bus.
You'll ................................................................................................................

g) I never felt comfortable when I was with them.
They always ......................................................................................................

h) I've heard a lot about you from Andrew.
Andrew ............................................................................................................

3   *Fill each of the blanks with a suitable word or phrase.*
EXAMPLE:  How often ....*do you go to the*.....cinema?

a) He joined his present company in 1972. By this time next year ..............................
........................................ fifteen years.

b) If I had listened to my mother, ...................................................................... such a
mess.

c) I'm afraid I can't lend you a pen, I .............................................................. on me.

d) Wish me luck, ............................................................ driving test tomorrow.

e) The chairman ................................................ any reference to the staff
changes.

f) She never takes .............................................................. I say.

4   *For each of the sentences below, write a new sentence* **as similar as possible in meaning to
the original sentence,** *but using the word given. This word must* **not be altered** *in any
way.*

EXAMPLE:  The large number of guests at his party was evidence of his
popularity.
**popular**
ANSWER:  *The large number of guests at his party showed how popular he
was.*

a) This bus is completely full up.
**left**

...................................................................................................................

b) He was jailed for two years.
   **sentence**

   .........................................................................................................................................................

c) I can't be bothered to write those letters today.
   **trouble**

   .........................................................................................................................................................

d) Have you done any teaching before?
   **job**

   .........................................................................................................................................................

e) You must arrive on time in the morning.
   **important**

   .........................................................................................................................................................

f) He is on a slimming diet.
   **weight**

   .........................................................................................................................................................

g) I hadn't arranged to meet them.
   **chance**

   .........................................................................................................................................................

h) With your blond hair you look like a Scandinavian.
   **pass**

   .........................................................................................................................................................

### SECTION B

5  *Read the following passage, then answer the questions which follow it.*

The first pseudo-Bond novel appeared four years after Ian Fleming's death: here, thirteen years later, is the second. At first this suggests, hearteningly, that James Bond has joined that small but select club of characters who have been brought back to life after the death of their creators simply because their readers want more of them. But
5  thirteen years is a long time, and during it there has been ample reason to fear that Bond had floated (literally at times) out of the world of fiction into that of cinematic fantasy, which is not quite the same thing. As everyone knows, the Bond novels were an adroit blend of realism and extravagance, and both were necessary: the one helped us to swallow the other. Because Sir Hugo Drax had red hair, one ear larger than the
10  other through plastic surgery, and wore a plain gold Patek Phillipe watch with a black leather strap, we accepted that his Moonraker rocket could blow London to bits. The Bond films, on the other hand, dispensed with the realism and concentrated on the extravagance, becoming exercises in camped-up absurdity. In this way there became two Bonds, book-Bond and film-Bond, each with his separate public. And a certain
15  hostility arose between them: for the readers, the films were ludicrous and childish travesties; the viewers, if they had ever heard of the books, saw them simply as material to be guyed, perhaps deservedly. . .
   Looking at the original canon after some twenty years confirms their almost mesmeric readability. . . How bad, and at the same time compellingly readable (his)
20  thrillers are! The pattern of all four that I have read is identical. Bond does not attract me, and that man with brains on ice and pitiless eye who organises the secret service in London seems to be a monument of ineptitude. Everything about Bond and his plans is known long before he arrives anywhere. But I cannot help reading on and there are rich satisfactions. . .

a)  What does the writter mean by 'the first pseudo-Bond novel' (line 1)?

    ....................................................................................................................................................

b)  What is the 'club' that it is suggested James Bond has joined (line 3)?

    ....................................................................................................................................................

c)  Why do you think the writer inserts the bracketed phrase '(literally at times)' (line 6)?

    ....................................................................................................................................................

d)  Explain the meaning of the phrase 'adroit blend' (line 8).

    ....................................................................................................................................................

e)  Why does the writer consider that the realism and extravagance in the Bond novels are both necessary (line 8)?

    ....................................................................................................................................................

f) What device in the Bond novels influences our acceptance of the evil intention of Sir Hugo Drax?

..................................................................................................................................................

g) What do you understand by the expression 'camped-up absurdity' (line 13)?

..................................................................................................................................................

h) What is the difference between 'book-Bond and film-Bond' (line 14)?

..................................................................................................................................................

i) What are the reasons for the hostility between readers and viewers of the Bond stories?

..................................................................................................................................................

j) Which phrase best describes the hypnotic attraction of the Bond novels?

..................................................................................................................................................

k) What is the writer's opinion of the literary style of the Bond novels?

..................................................................................................................................................

l) Why do you think the secret service organiser is referred to as a 'monument of ineptitude' (line 22)?

..................................................................................................................................................

m) In 70–100 words summarise the writer's views on the Bond novels and his enjoyment of them.

..................................................................................................................................................

..................................................................................................................................................

..................................................................................................................................................

..................................................................................................................................................

..................................................................................................................................................

# PAPER 4 LISTENING COMPREHENSION (Approx. 30 minutes)

*Further instructions will be given on the recording. Your answers must be written in ink in this booklet, using the spaces provided.*

## FIRST PART

*For questions 1–5 fill in the correct answer.*

| ① | Book title | |
|---|---|---|
| ② | Author | |
| ③ | When available | |
| ④ | Price | |
| ⑤ | Method of payment | |

*For questions 6–9, put a tick in one of the boxes A, B, C or D.*

6 Judging by his telephone call, MacDonald seems to be

    A over-anxious.

    B rather vague.

    C uninterested.

    D unintelligent.

| A |
|---|
| B |
| C |
| D |

7 He is ordering the book for

    A his tutor.

    B use in class.

    C personal pleasure.

    D a specific reason.

| A |
|---|
| B |
| C |
| D |

8 From the conversation we get the impression that MacDonald is

    A wary of his bank manager.

    B always in debt.

    C overdrawn at the bank.

    D uninterested in money.

| A |
|---|
| B |
| C |
| D |

9   Life at the student hostel would appear to be

   A   fairly uncomfortable.

   B   rather unfriendly.

   C   very homely.

   D   pretty easy-going.

| A |
|---|
| B |
| C |
| D |

## SECOND PART

*For questions 10–13 tick* **one** *of the boxes A, B, C or D.*

10   Harry is being interviewed by a

   A   police officer.

   B   social worker.

   C   radio reporter.

   D   newspaper columnist.

| A |
|---|
| B |
| C |
| D |

11   When Harry first saw him, he realised the boy

   A   was trying to row with one oar.

   B   had never done any rowing before.

   C   was an inexperienced oarsman.

   D   was having trouble with the oars.

| A |
|---|
| B |
| C |
| D |

12   What Harry did was particularly brave because he

   A   was not able to swim.

   B   had no experience of life-saving.

   C   was risking his own life.

   D   had not jumped from the bridge before.

| A |
|---|
| B |
| C |
| D |

13   From what Harry says we get the impression that he

   A   was embarrassed by the interviewer's questions.

   B   did not want to make much of the incident.

   C   could not really explain why he did it.

   D   wanted to forget the whole thing.

| A |
|---|
| B |
| C |
| D |

## THIRD PART

*For questions 14–22 you must write in the boxes what goods the shops specialise in or what types of shops they are. One has been done for you.*

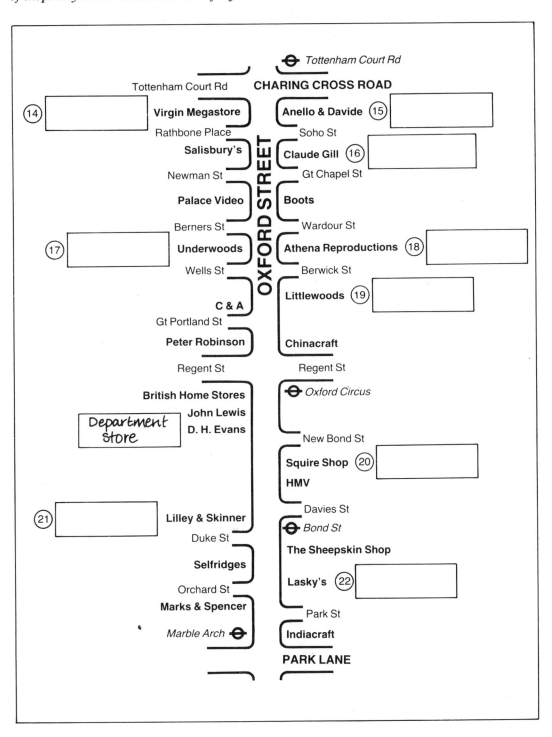

### FOURTH PART

*For questions 23–25 tick* **one** *of the boxes A, B, C or D.*

23   What is this speaker doing?

    A   Giving an election address.

    B   Reading a manifesto.

    C   Canvassing for votes.

    D   Nominating a candidate.

| A |
|---|
| B |
| C |
| D |

24   The political message of the Freedom for Youth party is that

    A   all voters must have fresh ideas.

    B   old policies must be rethought.

    C   words are more important than action.

    D   there must be change in society.

| A |
|---|
| B |
| C |
| D |

25   What the speaker says is likely to attract voters who are

    A   reactionary.

    B   idealistic.

    C   humanistic.

    D   anarchic.

| A |
|---|
| B |
| C |
| D |

# PAPER 5  INTERVIEW  (Approx. 15 minutes)

*Look at this photograph carefully and be prepared to describe and discuss it.*

a)  Describe the men.
            the weapons.
            the situation.

b)  Crime and violence.
    The use of firearms.
    The role of police in society.

c)  *Study one or more of the following passages and be prepared to answer questions or make comments on the subject matter.*

(i)  At least three people were injured last night in clashes between residents and security forces. Police and local officials fired tear gas, rubber bullets and bird-shot to disperse stone-throwing crowds. A policeman was injured when a petrol bomb was thrown into an armoured personnel carrier.

(ii)  I caught him as he was trying to cut through a vacant lot, and was beating the hell out of him when the car and the squad coppers got there, and one of them got each of us. One caught my coat from the back, pulled me away from Bobby, and slammed me against the side of the car with the flat of his hand.
'Break it up, punks,' he said. 'Down to the station for you.'
I wanted to kick out backward, but that wouldn't do any good so I started to talk fast.

(iii)   The saloon bars, leader columns and staffrooms of Britain have come up with many reasons for violence in the young: unemployment, materialistic values, the breakdown of domestic discipline, boredom. A less common suggestion is that we should look at the way we teach boys to be men. We must find a way of educating the peaceful side of the character of the male by valuing more highly the humanitarian values inherent in the arts and social sciences.

d)   General discussion:

*Study this cartoon and be prepared to describe it and comment on the underlying ideas.*

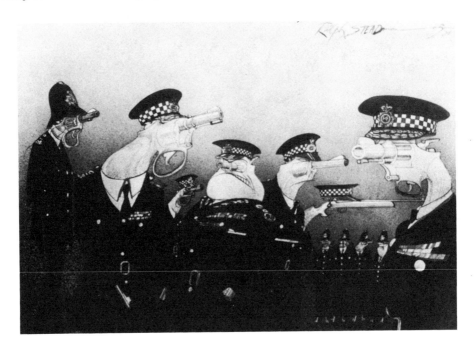

e)   Debate:

*Study the topic and be prepared to speak for or against the motion. One, or more, of the following themes may help you in the preparation of your speech(es).*

Topic:   **Violence in the world can only increase in the future.**
Themes:   Armed force is necessary to keep law and order.
Violence is an outlet for frustration.
Unemployment has resulted in bored, resentful young people.
Political, racial and religious unrest contribute.
Discussion can solve most problems.
Increased world poverty.
Importance of greater world understanding.

f)   (See Appendix: Prescribed texts)

# Test Two

## PAPER 1  READING COMPREHENSION  (1 hour)

*Answer all questions. Indicate your choice of answer in every case* **on the separate answer sheet** *already given out, which should show your name and examination index number. Follow carefully the instructions about how to record your answers. Give* **one answer only** *to each question. Marks will not be deducted for wrong answers: your total score on this test will be the number of correct answers you give.*

### SECTION A

*In this section you must choose the word or phrase which best completes each sentence.* **On your answer sheet** *indicate the letter A, B, C or D against the number of each item 1 to 25 for the word or phrase you choose.*

1  The courtroom was extremely crowded and the atmosphere was ................. .
   A burning    B stifling    C blazing    D roasting

2  It is impossible for us to ................. all your demands.
   A attest to    B admit to    C avow to    D accede to

3  Unless we take immediate precautions, we shall not be able to ................. the epidemic.
   A contain    B hold    C staunch    D destroy

4  These figures will give you a ................. estimate of the cost of the goods.
   A superficial    B rough    C scant    D short

5  Even as a young man, my father was always very ................. .
   A untypical    B dissident    C eccentric    D uncharacteristic

6  After half an hour the meeting ................. in confusion.
   A broke out    B broke off    C broke away    D broke up

7  The ................. are still holding thirty people hostage on the plane.
   A bandits    B hijackers    C kidnappers    D guerrillas

8  If you send the letter here, my mother will ................. it to my new address.
   A transmit    B forward    C transfer    D advance

9  I didn't really understand the ................. of his argument.
   A matter    B scope    C tenor    D gist

10  The label said 'It is dangerous to ................. the stated dose'.
   A overdo    B exceed    C infringe    D repeat

11 He made no attempt to ............... his extraordinary behaviour.
   A vindicate    B justify    C manifest    D exonerate

12 At many restaurants a service ............... is included in the bill.
   A charge    B tip    C tax    D gratuity

13 The Speaker at the House of Commons was interrupted by boos from the ............... of the House.
   A ground    B platform    C floor    D arena

14 There are no such things ............... ghosts.
   A similar to    B like    C same as    D as

15 The approach to the temple was ............... with marble.
   A faced    B plated    C coated    D paved

16 I don't believe a further reduction in income tax is within the ............... of possibility.
   A bounds    B limits    C confines    D borders

17 We must remind you that the terms of the contract are legally ............... .
   A obligatory    B liable    C ethical    D binding

18 It's no ............... of his how I choose to spend my money.
   A affair    B responsibility    C business    D liability

19 That notice says there is no admission except to ............... personnel.
   A legitimate    B authorised    C approved    D lawful

20 On examination by experts, the picture turned out to be a ............... .
   A fake    B sham    C fraud    D fabrication

21 He speaks quite good English, ............... he's never had any lessons.
   A since    B in spite of    C although    D nevertheless

22 The only ............... was that there was no air-conditioning in the hotel.
   A hitch    B catch    C fault    D snag

23 Peter was ............... from hospital last Wednesday.
   A released    B discharged    C withdrawn    D dismissed

24 The poor reception on your TV is probably due to outside ............... .
   A interference    B intervention    C interruption    D interception

25 As hard as she tried, she ............... couldn't understand the question.
   A yet    B still    C even    D always

## SECTION B

*In this section you will find after each of the passages a number of questions or unfinished statements about the passage, each with four suggested answers or ways of finishing. You must choose the one you think fits best according to the passage.* **On your answer sheet** *indicate the letter A, B, C or D against the number of each item 26 to 40 for the answer you choose. Give* **one answer only** *to each question. Read each passage right through before choosing your answers.*

## FIRST PASSAGE

Interest is steadily spreading from a minority of enthusiasts in developing renewable sources of energy – wind, wave and solar power, tidal and geothermal energy. Additional support for them has come with a proposal to explore the untapped sources of hydro-electric power in Scotland.

The details are presented by Mr William Manser in a study called 'The Case for an Inquiry into Hydro-electric Generation in the North of Scotland'. He calls for an expert committee to look at the developments possible for hydro-electric sites and, more important, for means of financing them.

There is a clear industrial connection in Mr Manser's study because it was done for the Federation of Civil Engineering Contractors; hydro-electric schemes, by definition, have a large civil engineering component in them. Mr Manser estimates that wind power could theoretically provide more than 7 per cent of electricity supply in the United Kingdom, provided suitable sites for generators could be found. However, the practical viability of wind power generation is not likely to be understood until 1990.

Other developments using renewable energy sources are also at an early stage as far as their commercial possibilities are concerned, he believes.

The best developed and most suitable form of renewable energy is in his view, hydro power. The technology has been developed over centuries and is still progressing. At present it is the cheapest form of electricity generation.

Mr Manser examined past surveys of the north of Scotland and identified several as suitable for hydro-electric generation. Those are in the remote areas, usually of great natural beauty.

But Mr Manser says a well designed dam can be impressive in itself. It is also possible to make installations as unobtrusive as possible, to the point of burying parts of them. Hydro generation involves no water pollution, smoke creation or unsightly stocking-out yards.

The main trouble, it appears from his report, is financing an undertaking which has a heavy initial capital cost, and very low running costs.

However, Mr Manser does not see that as an unfamiliar position for the electricity industry. He cites the proposed construction of the new nuclear power station at Sizewell in Suffolk, which will have a high initial capital cost.

The argument at Sizewell that the reason for the expenditure is that the capital will provide a benefit in lower costs and higher returns in the long-term, applies equally to hydro-electric generation.

26  The main subject of this passage is the
    A  conservation of energy.
    B  high costs of energy sources.
    C  recycling of resources.
    D  energy generated by water power.

27  From the passage we understand that Mr Manser's study was
    A  presented by a financial committee.
    B  part of a civil engineering contract.
    C  commissioned by a professional organisation.
    D  written in conjunction with an expert committee.

28  What drawback is there to the provision of wind power generation?
    A  The supply method is not yet understood.
    B  It's a non-viable proposition.
    C  There is a lack of suitable sites.
    D  Theoretical application is still needed.

29  The advantage of hydro-electric power is that it
    A  does not damage the environment.
    B  is relatively easy to install.
    C  requires little or no maintenance.
    D  is more suitable for remote areas.

30  In Mr Manser's opinion, the main stumbling block to the development of hydro-electric power is the
    A  capital outlay.
    B  running costs.
    C  public expenditure.
    D  financial risk.

## SECOND PASSAGE

Computers? Give me a pocket calculator and I'd show you how to burn it out in five minutes. I belong to a simpler age, probably the Stone one. No, you can keep your computers, indeed, anyone who strikes a blow against them gets my vote, like this chap.

When he was told that a cut-back in estimated production the following year would lead to his being given the push, a computer programmer working for a large American corporation provided a timely lesson to all who don't want their departure from the ranks of the employed to pass unnoticed.

He was told that he would have to go at the end of the year. For the final few months he worked like a dog and no one could have suspected the little ploy he was working up. He went to the office Christmas party as usual and even sent cards to his colleagues, and when the time came for his farewell party his head of department made a moving tribute to his 'industry'. He told the programmer how sorry he would be to lose his services and said that no one would forget the time he'd spent working with them. He probably never spoke a truer word in his life.

The department's work load had eased off just before the Christmas break and no one took too much notice of the routine programmes that were fed into the main computer. It was then that our man struck. While he was feeding the computer with a series of standard instructions, he slipped in an extra one, scheduled for 31 December, 'erase all records', it read.

31  The passage reveals that the writer
   A  approved of the programmer's action.
   B  was extremely adept with a pocket calculator.
   C  disapproved of corporate American companies.
   D  was completely indifferent to computers.

32  The company's reason for dismissing the computer programmer was
   A  increased production costs.
   B  a lower profit margin.
   C  a planned decrease in output.
   D  alternative production methods.

33  What did the computer programmer decide to do when he was given notice?
   A  Put the company out of business.
   B  Get his own back.
   C  Expose the company's inefficiency.
   D  Get his job back.

34  What did the employee programme the computer to do?
   A  Record false information.
   B  Recycle the records.
   C  Erase its memory bank.
   D  Cease to store information.

35  The writer's approach to his subject is
   A  humorous.
   B  cynical.
   C  sarcastic.
   D  satirical.

## THIRD PASSAGE

*Extract 1*

Well then, the table should be shaped like the full moon – symbol of married bliss and happy family life, the table top, that round arena of contented companionship, being at its loveliest when black in colour and of highly polished Szechuan lacquer.

The table should be covered with a white, a snow-white tablecloth; and if, at the end of the banquet, the tablecloth carries evidence of each of the courses, that is only to be rejoiced at. After all, those who really enjoy their food do not guard their movements like the actors of mime but pick and soak, take and scoop up with impatient speed as they endeavour to transfer the morsels to their own rice bowl. It is therefore an honour to the cook as well as to the host. . .

*Extract 2*

In our decorations we must not forget the dining-room table when our guests gather round it. A very pretty centrepiece is made by covering an inverted basin with moss, into which insert sprigs of holly quite thick until it forms a pyramid of holly. On the top place a figure of Old Father Christmas (which may be brought at any bazaar or sugar-plum shop), and instead of the holly sprig he generally holds in his hand, place a spray of mistletoe. A great many lights are required, where fir and holly are much used, in table decoration, otherwise the effect is heavy and gloomy.

These hints will make it easy to adorn the house for Christmas; but half the pleasure consists in inventing new devices, and giving scope to one's taste and ingenuity, new ideas springing up and developing themselves as the occasion arises, till the worker finds delight in the work, and thus best rewarded for the toil.

*Extract 3*

'But apart from our work in the gardens and in the stovehouses we had a definite daily routine connected with the house. We had to change the flowers in the various rooms, in the hall, in the drawing-room, in her ladyship's boudoir and so on; and, most important of all, we had to decorate the dining-table. For breakfast and lunch there were three little plant pots on the table. Dinner was at 8 p.m.; and at 7 o'clock you had to decorate the tablecloth. But first you had to find out from the butler what silver he was going to use. We made a pattern of leaves and flowers on the tablecloth and we had to know where the silver was going to lie before you did this. I recollect a herring-bone pattern I used to fancy; and I carried out this design very often. One of the most important things we had to watch out for was that the flowers didn't obstruct the view of the guests. It wouldn't have done to have that. Next morning the flowers had to be taken off the table well before breakfast-time.'

*Extract 4*

The dining-car was certainly unchanged. On each table there still ceremoniously stood two opulent black bottles of some unthinkable wine, false pledges of conviviality. They were never opened and rarely dusted. They may contain ink, they may contain the elixir of life. I do not know. I doubt if anyone does.

Lavish but faded paper frills still clustered coyly round the pots of paper flowers, from whose sad petals the dust of two continents perpetually threatened the specific gravity of the soup. The lengthy and trilingual menu had not been revised; 75 per cent of the dishes were still apocryphal, all the prices were exorbitant. The cruet, as before, was of interest rather to the geologist than to the gourmet. Coal dust from the Donetz Basin, tiny flakes of granite from the Urals, sand whipped by the wind all the way from the Gobi Desert – what a fascinating story that salt-cellar could have told under the microscope!

36   What do extracts 3 and 4 have in common?
    A   A feeling of discontentment.
    B   A type of table decoration.
    C   The significance of objects on the table.
    D   An effect of unbroken tradition.

37   The writer of extract 1
    A   agrees with the viewpoint of extract 2.
    B   criticises people who do not enjoy eating.
    C   emphasises the enjoyment of food.
    D   shows that the table decoration is vital.

38   The first 3 extracts all agree that table decoration should be
    A   elaborate.
    B   appropriate.
    C   symbolic.
    D   original.

39   Extracts 1, 2 and 3 share the opinion that
    A   eating should be a pleasurable experience.
    B   decorating the table is more important than the food.
    C   the feelings of the host or hostess are of prime importance.
    D   guests get as much pleasure from the appearance of the tables as from the food.

40   Extract 4 describes a scene in
    A   a large country house.
    B   a restaurant.
    C   a train.
    D   an aeroplane.

# PAPER 2 COMPOSITION (2 hours)

*Write **two only** of the following composition exercises. Your answers must follow exactly the instructions given. Write in pen, not pencil. You are allowed to make alterations, but see that your work is clear and easy to read.*

1 Describe a musician or singer whose work you enjoy. (About 350 words)

2 'Sex discrimination still exists in society.' Discuss. (About 350 words)

3 Write a story entitled 'The Lucky Mascot'. (About 350 words)

4 Write sets of instructions explaining *two* of the following, using about 150 words for each.
> How to drive a car.
> How to swim.
> How to make a good cup of coffee (not instant).
> How to amuse a child of 5 for a day.

5 (See Appendix: Prescribed texts)

## PAPER 3   USE OF ENGLISH   (2 hours)

*Answer* **all** *the questions.*
*Your answers must be written in ink in this booklet, using the spaces provided.*

### SECTION A

1   *Fill each of the numbered blanks in the following passage with* **one** *suitable word.*

The ..................... (1) of the Panacolour Painting Competition for young artists
..................... (2) the age of 18, is Kathleen Salt, ..................... (3) 15 of Harben, Kent.
Kathleen's entry was a study of seabirds ..................... (4) above the beach in an
approaching storm. The judges agreed that the painting ..................... (5) the feeling
of isolation ..................... (6) with such a scene and that the sombre ..................... (7)
of the clouds ..................... (8) in the distance contrasted perfectly ..................... (9)
the pale ..................... (10) of the winter sun. 'We were ..................... (11),' said Mark
Parsons, Managing ..................... (12) of Panacolour, 'to receive an entry which was
not ..................... (13) another pretty ..................... (14) of a dog or a garden.
Kathleen's work shows ..................... (15) promise and we hope that ..................... (16)
this prize will encourage her to go ..................... (17) with her studies.' Kathleen will
receive the first ..................... (18) of £250 and her painting will be ..................... (19)
in the Harben Art ..................... (20) next month.

2   *Finish each of the following sentences in such a way that it means exactly the same as the*
*sentence printed before it.*

      EXAMPLE:   He didn't seem to want to leave.

      ANSWER:   He seemed *to want to stay*.

   a)   I don't think he has much chance of getting the job.
      I doubt .....................................................................................

   b)   He doesn't always tell the truth.
      You shouldn't .....................................................................................

   c)   His salary is under £6,000 a year.
      He earns .....................................................................................

   d)   I was at a loss to know what to do.
      I couldn't .....................................................................................

e) Antiques don't interest me very much.
I'm not ..................................................................................................................

f) There was an uproar at the end of the meeting.
The meeting ..........................................................................................................

g) A large number of people have tried to salvage the treasure.
Numerous attempts ............................................................................................

h) Why did he say that?
What ...............................................................................................................?

3 *Fill each of the blanks with a suitable word or phrase.*

EXAMPLE:  If I'd been you, *I wouldn't have been* so keen to go to dinner.

a) Excuse me, but ........................... my seat.

b) I should take those books out of your suitcase, or ........................... heavy.

c) Are we ........................... fish and chips for supper?

d) I think you ........................... a doctor if you don't feel any better tomorrow.

e) He ........................... spoken to you like that.

f) Shall ........................... the tea, or will you?

g) You've ........................... lies again, you naughty boy.

4 *For each of the sentences below, write a new sentence* **as similar as possible in meaning to the original sentence,** *but using the word given. This word must* **not be altered** *in any way.*

EXAMPLE:  He borrowed ten pounds from Chris.
**lent**

ANSWER:  *Chris lent him ten pounds.*
........................................................................................................

a) This is the last opportunity you will ever have of hearing this great singer.
**never**

........................................................................................................

b) No one else could make the decision for me.
**up**

........................................................................................................

c) I don't think we will ever find a solution to this problem.
**solving**

........................................................................................................

d)   He wasn't fit to drive.
     **condition**

     ......................................................................................................................................

e)   Didn't she say she was sorry she kept you waiting?
     **apologise**

     ......................................................................................................................................

f)   As soon as I got to Heathrow, I telephoned my office.
     **first**

     ......................................................................................................................................

g)   The violence at the match was out of hand.
     **control**

     ......................................................................................................................................

h)   Was there anything about his new boss in his letter?
     **say**

     ......................................................................................................................................

### SECTION B

5  *Read the following passage, and then answer the questions that follow it.*

In the days when train travel was the norm, we were all rather inclined to take it for granted. After a thirty-year glut of jet and motorway travel, the novelty of which has long since worn off, we can see that train travel was – and when you can get it, still is – comparative bliss. No one who has travelled long distances on a motorway, chained
5  like a dog to his seat, unable to read or drink, blocked by juggernauts from the passing view, deafened by their engines and blackened by their fumes, would wish to repeat the experience for pleasure.

Air travel is little better. One is cramped and disorientated. Chains are *de rigueur* here too; and if you happen to find yourself next to a manic child or compulsive
10  chatterbox, there is little you can do to escape. Airlines attempt to compensate for these deficiencies with piped music, films, and instant alcohol. These overload the system and, combined with a swingeing time-change, lead to total dysfunction; arriving within hours of setting out, one needs two days to recover.

Train journeys, in comparison, have much to offer. Unlike sea or air travel, one has
15  a fair notion where one is; and the countryside, like a moving picture show, unrolls itself before one's eyes. One is transported in comfort, even style, to the wild places of earth – forest, mountain, desert; and always there is the counterpoint between life within the train and life without. . .

One can move around in a train, visit the buffet for snacks or a drink, play cards (or,
20  on some American trains, the piano), strike up a conversation, read, sleep, snore, make love. Luggage is to hand too, not as in a car or airplane, ungetatable in trunk or belly.

Some trains are designed to satisfy national needs. The American club car, for instance, exists for passengers to bore each other with accounts of business deals,
25  marital problems, extramarital affairs: the price they know they must pay is to be bored in turn later. The English have never gone in for club cars, believing that on long journeys one should not utter at all. When buffet cars were first introduced to British trains, there was a real danger they might lead to social intercourse. Happily they turned out to be so utterly bereft of comfort and style, so perennially awash in
30  soldiers and beer, as to discourage any right-thinking person from staying a moment longer than the time needed for his purchase, which he is then free to convey to the privacy and silence of his seat.

Yet the sweetest pleasure of any long train journey lies in its anticipation. . . Even if achievement rarely matches promise, one may still daydream. How green are the
35  vistas, what's for dinner, whom shall I meet? In the end it's the passengers who provide the richest moments of any long-distance trip. For train travel, being constricted both in time and space, magnifies character, intensifies relationships, unites the disparate. Ordinary people become extra-ordinary, larger than life; and in the knowledge that they will not meet again, expansive, confiding, intimate. Let us
40  talk now, you and I: later will be too late.

a)  Why is a word like 'glut' used in connection with jet and motorway travel (line 2)?

    ....................................................................................................................................

b) Describe the 'comparative bliss' (line 4).

.................................................................................................................................................

c) Explain the metaphor 'chained like a dog' (lines 4–5) in this context.

.................................................................................................................................................

d) What are the disadvantages of air travel according to the writer?

.................................................................................................................................................

e) What leads to 'total dysfunction' (line 12)?

.................................................................................................................................................

f) Why is the countryside compared to 'a moving picture show' (line 15)?

.................................................................................................................................................

g) Explain, in your own words, 'counterpoint' (line 17)?

.................................................................................................................................................

h) What is meant by 'ungetatable in trunk or belly' (lines 21–22)?

.................................................................................................................................................

i) What are the American national needs?

.................................................................................................................................................

j) Why do the English dislike club cars?

.................................................................................................................................................

k) Explain the disadvantages of buffet cars.

.................................................................................................................................................

l) What is the meaning of the phrase 'utterly bereft' (line 29)?

.................................................................................................................................................

m) Why does the writer think the passengers on train journeys provide the most interest?

.................................................................................................................................................

n) In 50–60 words summarise the writer's views on the advantages of train journeys over other forms of travel.

.................................................................................................................................................

.................................................................................................................................................

.................................................................................................................................................

.................................................................................................................................................

.................................................................................................................................................

# PAPER 4 LISTENING COMPREHENSION (Approx. 30 minutes)

*Further instructions will be given on the recording. Your answers must be written in ink in this booklet, using the spaces provided.*

## FIRST PART

*For questions 1–5, put a tick in one of the boxes A, B, C or D.*

1 The customer is enquiring about

  A hiring a car abroad.

  B having his car serviced.

  C leaving his car in the UK.

  D parking his car abroad.

| A |
|---|
| B |
| C |
| D |

2 The clerk informs the customer that he must pay

  A the minimum rate.

  B a fixed charge.

  C the list price.

  D a standing order.

| A |
|---|
| B |
| C |
| D |

3 What time should Mr Brown deliver his car to Gatwick Motors?

  A 11.30

  B 11.20

  C 11.10

  D 11.00

| A |
|---|
| B |
| C |
| D |

4 How does the customer react to the number of questions he has to answer?

  A Rather impatiently.

  B Very relaxedly.

  C Extremely angrily.

  D Completely indifferently.

| A |
|---|
| B |
| C |
| D |

5   The customer leaves in a hurry in order to avoid

    A   losing his parking space.

    B   seeing the traffic warden.

    C   losing his licence.

    D   being fined.

| |
|---|
| A |
| B |
| C |
| D |

## SECOND PART

*For questions 6–15 tick whether you think the statements are true or false.*

| | True | False |
|---|---|---|
| 6   Salisbury Cathedral is a fine example of early Medieval architecture. | | |
| 7   It is possible to see how far the spire leans from the vertical by studying marks on the Cathedral floor. | | |
| 8   Additional columns were added to support the tower and spire in the 14th and 15th centuries. | | |
| 9   Sir Christopher Wren designed a building to be used as a hospital for the clergy. | | |
| 10   Plans of the Cathedral could be found at the front of the bookstall. | | |
| 11   The nave is 449 feet long. | | |
| 12   The Earl of Salisbury signed the Magna Carta in 1215. | | |
| 13   St. Osmund was able to cure the diseased limbs of the pilgrims. | | |
| 14   The Salisbury document was originally housed in the library at Old Sarum. | | |
| 15   The ordinary people of England were first given some control over their own affairs in 1215. | | |

### THIRD PART

*For questions 16–18, write your answers in the spaces provided.*

16   You wish to buy a Senior Citizen Railcard but have to produce proof that you are over 60. What documents are valid proof?

   (i)   ........................................................................................................................................

   (ii)  ........................................................................................................................................

   (iii) ........................................................................................................................................

17   Two types of railcard are issued, valued £12 and £7 respectively. What reductions do you get on the £12 card?

   (i)   ........................................................................................................................................

   (ii)  ........................................................................................................................................

18   There are three other benefits obtained by possessing a railcard, what are they?

   (i)   ........................................................................................................................................

   (ii)  ........................................................................................................................................

   (iii) ........................................................................................................................................

### FOURTH PART

*For questions 19–22, tick **one** of the boxes A, B, C or D.*

19   Who is the programme mainly intended for?

   A   Commuters.

   B   Early risers.

   C   Shift workers.

   D   Insomniacs.

| A |
| B |
| C |
| D |

20   What would best describe 'Night Bus'?

   A   A quiz programme.

   B   A guessing game.

   C   A crossword puzzle.

   D   A music competition.

| A |
| B |
| C |
| D |

12  To take part in 'Night Bus' you have to

    A   choose a Caribbean island.

    B   solve certain clues.

    C   find different routes.

    D   go to several places.

| A |
|---|
| B |
| C |
| D |

22  To enter the competition you have to

    A   go personally to Victoria.

    B   phone Steve Holly.

    C   send a postcard each night.

    D   write in to Radio Metro.

| A |
|---|
| B |
| C |
| D |

# PAPER 5  INTERVIEW  (Approx. 15 minutes)

*Look at this photograph carefully and be prepared to describe and discuss it.*

a)   Describe  the group of young people.
               the old man.
               what the people are doing.

b)   Fashion.
    The generation gap.
    Changing attitudes in society.

c)   *Study one or more of the following passages and be prepared to answer questions or make comments on the subject matter.*

(i)   They were a group of young people who pass their time on the sometimes bleak but not always hostile streets. As dropouts from the common scramble for success, they relate to one another with warmth, kindliness and humour. In contrast, the older members of their neighbourhood, treat life warily and lead essentially lonely lives.

(ii)   Already, punk's tenth birthday has provoked an outpouring of sentimentality and nostalgia, an opportunity for the pundits who came of age in the crucible to relive their glorious adolescence, and possibly wonder where it all went. An opportunity for everyone else to wonder whether it was all really so important in the first place. After all, punk may have been rude and unruly, but it always testified more ardently to the hardy perennial notion of a good time than it did to revolutionary change.

(iii)   'Old age is not for cowards.' The old man looks angrily at the young people, as if they cannot possibly understand. 'I have no illusions. It is not going to get any better. I know what I have to go through. Don't think I don't. You wake up some mornings and you don't know where the hell you are. Just like a child. Everything is in the fog. Some days it lifts. Some days it doesn't.'

d)   General discussion:

*Study this leaflet about sheltered housing for elderly people and be prepared to give your opinion about the relative merits of looking after the elderly in the family, in sheltered housing or in a residential old peoples' home.*

# Sheltered Housing

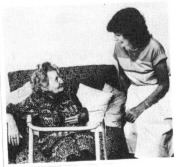

## Sheltered Housing

Sheltered housing is designed for elderly people but is **not** an elderly people's home. Tenants have their own individual flats and normally look after themselves but there is a warden on hand to give advice and help in emergencies. There are usually extra facilities available like a laundry or common room which everyone is encouraged to use.

## The Warden

The warden provides a 9–5, Monday–Friday service for tenants. The warden usually has an office where tenants can drop in for advice but a daily visit will be made to tenants if necessary. Wardens cannot be expected to carry out day-to-day tasks for tenants, such as housework or shopping, neither can they provide nursing care. However they can help to arrange for services such as home helps and meals on wheels to be provided by the Social Services Department.

## Emergencies

Every flat is linked to the warden by an alarm system. In an emergency, such as a sudden illness or after a fall, a tenant can call the warden using one of the pull-cords installed in every flat. The warden will then try to contact a doctor, ambulance or the social services, as well as friends or relatives of the tenant. To help the warden act quickly in an emergency, names and addresses of the tenant's doctor and nearest relatives should be given to the warden. If any of these names and addresses change, the warden should be told immediately. The warden should also be told about any specific medical problems such as diabetes, high blood pressure or angina and whether the tenant is taking any medicines. Some wardens keep a set of master keys to every flat in their block to use in an emergency, but where this is not the case, tenants should let their warden have a spare key for emergencies. If a tenant changes the locks, a new spare key should be given to the warden, otherwise valuable time could be lost in an emergency.

*and/or*

e) Debate:

*Study the topic and be prepared to speak for or against the motion. One, or more, of the following themes may help you in the preparation of your speech(es).*

Topic:     **There should be more co-operation between the young and the elderly.**
Themes:   Youth community service.
           Car day trips for elderly – volunteer youth service.
           Doing shopping for elderly.
           Recording oral tradition of elderly.
           Elderly baby-sitting for young.
           Elderly experience can help the young.
           Classes for elderly and young – learning together.

f)   (See Appendix: Prescribed texts)

## PAPER 1   READING COMPREHENSION   (1 hour)

*Answer all questions. Indicate your choice of answer in every case* **on the separate answer sheet** *already given out, which should show your name and examination index number. Follow carefully the instructions about how to record your answers. Give* **one answer only** *to each question. Marks will not be deducted for wrong answers: your total score on this test will be the number of correct answers you give.*

### SECTION A

*In this section you must choose the word or phrase which best completes each sentence.* **On your answer sheet** *indicate the letter A, B, C or D against the number of each item 1 to 25 for the word or phrase you choose.*

1   Five hundred men at the car factory will be made ................ at the end of the month.
   A unemployed   B redundant   C expendable   D inoperative

2   The young offender was placed on ................ for a year.
   A trial   B surveillance   C probation   D charge

3   The possibility of an autumn election cannot be ................ .
   A struck out   B left out   C ruled out   D counted out

4   Most road accidents are caused by ................ error.
   A human   B man-made   C personal   D mortal

5   He was ................ to explain the sudden fall in profit.
   A in the dark   B in two minds   C out of touch   D at a loss

6   She became ................ British citizen in 1980.
   A an immigrant   B a naturalised   C a converted   D a national

7   Did you see that ................ about wildlife in Australia on television last night?
   A soap opera   B history   C situational comedy   D documentary

8   He alleged that his phone had been ................ by the police.
   A tapped   B connected   C planted   D encoded

9   There is no point in our continuing to argue ................ .
   A wide of the mark   B off target   C at cross purposes   D far from the truth

40

10  What you do in your spare time is nothing to ................. me.
    A  bear·upon    B  interest    C  do with    D  concern

11  The speaker ................. so low that I could hardly hear him.
    A  jabbered    B  mumbled    C  gabbled    D  grumbled

12  Have you ................. your holiday yet?
    A  set up    B  fixed up    C  tied up    D  taken up

13  I always take ................. aspirin when I have a headache.
    A  molten    B  soluble    C  fluid    D  runny

14  She didn't know ................. to turn for financial help.
    A  who    B  what    C  where    D  how

15  The culture of ................. minorities living in our society must be respected.
    A  tribal    B  racial    C  national    D  native

16  These paintings did not come to ................. until after the artist's death.
    A  sight    B  light    C  range    D  view

17  The police ................. off the street where the bomb had gone off.
    A  sealed    B  battened    C  shuttered    D  fastened

18  A national ................. shows that 65% of the population would prefer to live in a city.
    A  quiz    B  inquiry    C  examination    D  survey

19  I have not the faintest ................. why he resigned.
    A  idea    B  thought    C  concept    D  opinion

20  In the past, steel ................. for 30% of UK exports.
    A  totalled    B  amounted    C  accounted    D  reached

21  After the fire a gang of youths ................. the store.
    A  purloined    B  burgled    C  ransacked    D  pilfered

22  'I'm afraid that the book is out of ................., sir. I could try to get it for you.'
    A  stock    B  order    C  store    D  supply

23  You should take notice of warnings that state that guard dogs are on ................. .
    A  defence    B  alert    C  watch    D  patrol

24  We must take ................. to see that the same mistake doesn't occur again.
    A  moves    B  steps    C  ways    D  means

25  I ................. his telephone number while he was still talking.
    A  wrote up    B  jotted down    C  set down    D  dashed off

### SECTION B

*In this section you will find after each of the passages a number of questions or unfinished statements about the passage, each with four suggested answers or ways of finishing. You must choose the one you think fits best according to the passage.* **On your answer sheet** *indicate the letter A, B, C or D against the number of each item 26 to 40 for the answer you choose. Give* **one answer only** *to each question. Read each passage right through before choosing your answers.*

## FIRST PASSAGE

For anyone who is set on a career in fashion it is not enough to have succeeded in college. The real test is whether they can survive and become established during their early 20s making a name for themselves in the real world where business skills can count for as much as flair and creativity. . .

Fashion is a hard business. There is a continuous amount of stress because work is at a constant breakneck speed to prepare for the next season's collections. It is extremely competitive and there is the constant need to cultivate good coverage in newspapers and magazines. It also requires continual freshness because the appetite for new ideas is insatiable. 'We try to warn people before they come to us about how tough it is,' says Lydia Kemeny, the Head of Fashion at St. Martin's School of Art in London, 'and we point out that drive and determination are essential.'

This may seem far removed from the popular image of trendy and dilettante young people spending their time designing pretty dresses. That may well be what they do in their first year of study but a good college won't be slow in introducing students to commercial realities. 'We don't stamp on the blossoming flower of creativity but in the second year we start introducing the constraints of price, manufacturability, marketing and so on.'

Almost all fashion design is done to a brief. It is not a form of self-expression as such, although there is certainly room for imagination and innovation. Most young designers are going to end up as employees of a manufacturer or fashion house and they still need to be able to work within the characteristic style of their employer. Even those students who are most avant-garde in their own taste of clothes and image may need to adapt to produce designs which are right for the mainstream Marks and Spencer type of market. They also have to be able to work at both the exclusively expensive and the cheap end of the market and the challenge to produce good design inexpensively may well be more demanding than where money is no object.

26  To be successful as a fashion designer you must

    A  have excellent academic qualifications.

    B  be able to handle business problems.

    C  be well established before you are 20.

    D  have taken an intensive commercial course.

27 All fashion designers should expect to

 A cope with continual fatigue.

 B make a rapid turnover.

 C work without remission.

 D face tough competition.

28 In fashion design one of the most important factors is to

 A satisfy excessive demands.

 B maintain good press contacts.

 C make instant decisions.

 D cultivate public taste.

29 Training must acquaint the student with a knowledge of

 A marketing techniques.

 B fashion economics.

 C factory management.

 D trading patterns.

30 Initially, many young designers have to

 A work for department stores.

 B change their personal taste in fashion.

 C repress their creativity.

 D conform to a certain image.

31 The views on fashion design expressed in this article

 A present an encouraging picture.

 B contain some innovative ideas.

 C dispel some common illusions.

 D discount the creative element.

## SECOND PASSAGE

English language teaching, like any other teaching, involves unequal status and unequal power. Teachers, with the weight of their employers and possibly a whole national system behind them, can establish rules of behaviour and interaction in the classroom which are unlike those that operate between people in the world outside. A look at any of the classroom language transcribed since observational research began reveals great differences between classroom communication between teachers and students and real-world communication between individuals (even where there is a great age or authority gap). Thus, it is particularly important that teachers should ask themselves from time to time: 'How justified are we in treating learners the way we do? Are we guilty of an insensitive abuse of power?'.

. . . The fact that foreign-language learning, particularly at the early stages, can involve language production and communication reminiscent of the early stages of mother-tongue development (and thus of infancy) makes it doubly important that teachers be on their guard against viewing the learner, and not only the adult learner, as 'child-like' or in need of concessions normally (and often unnecessarily) made to infants or young children. It is, of course, hard to remember, particularly for native speakers, that someone who can cope with only very basic communication in the target language is in fact already fully competent as a communicator in at least one language, and that, even if the way in which things are communicated must necessarily be simple, what is communicated and what is referred to needs no more simplification than it would if there were no difference in language ability between student and teacher.

32  Teachers are able to establish their own rules in the classroom because they

    A  have a high professional status.

    B  have support from outside authorities.

    C  think the classroom is different from the outside world.

    D  don't operate in the same way as other people.

33  Research into classroom communication shows that the biggest difference in language usage occurs

    A  when there is a large generation gap.

    B  in teacher-student interaction.

    C  between people in authority and their subordinates.

    D  among individuals inside and outside the classroom.

34  When teaching a foreign language it is advisable to

A   communicate on a childish level.

B   make concessions as in mother-tongue teaching.

C   make allowances for the learner's immaturity.

D   respect the learner's innate ability.

35  A major problem facing the foreign language learner is how to

A   understand complicated problems.

B   express complex ideas in simple language.

C   simplify sophisticated concepts.

D   state a simple idea in an elaborate way.

THIRD PASSAGE

# See all the sights with us

There's so much to see and do in London, you'll want to get around as easily (and cheaply) as possible.
The very best way is by London Transport.
Here's some ideas to be getting on with.

**A The London Explorer**
Buy one and forget about queueing for tickets each time you travel. You get unlimited travel on the Underground and buses for 1.3, 4 or 7 days plus a free mini-guide to London and valuable discount vouchers.

**B Guided Coach Tours**
See (and learn about) all the sights in comfort. Destinations include the City and West End. Windsor. Hampton Court and Stratford. Pick up a brochure and book your seat at any London Transport Travel Information Centre and in most hotels.
Fully qualified guides.

**C The Official London Sightseeing Tour**
The best tour around! 18 miles and 1½ hours of London's finest sights. All on a genuine red London bus. Pick up from 4 convenient points—Baker Street Station, Victoria, Marble Arch and Piccadilly Circus. Guided and Unguided tours, pay on the bus or tickets in advance at a discount from any Travel Information Centre.

**D Heathrow? We go!...**
**by Underground and Airbus**
The Piccadilly Line runs between Central London and Heathrow every few minutes, journey time about 40 minutes. Serves all the main hotel areas.
Airbus is ideal if you've lots of luggage or like to see the sights while travelling. Three routes pick up at 18 points throughout Central London and serve all 3 terminals.

Our Tourist Information Folder will give you full details of all the extra special tourist services we offer—ask for your free copy at any Underground station or at the Travel Information Centres at Heathrow, Piccadilly Circus, Oxford Circus, St. James's Park, King's Cross and Victoria.

**BUS & TUBE**
**01-222 1234**
*24hr INFORMATION*

36 Which London Transport service, A, B, C or D, would give you the opportunity of the most comprehensive round trip of London?

37 If you are heavily loaded, which service would you use? A, B, C or D.

38 On which service, A, B, C or D, could you go where you liked?

39 You have only a short time, but would like a guided tour. Which service do you use? A, B, C or D.

40 The aim of this advertisement is to

A encourage more people to explore London.

B get more people to use public transport.

C persuade more people to buy tourist tickets.

D help more people to understand London Transport.

# PAPER 2 COMPOSITION (2 hours)

*Write* **two only** *of the following composition exercises. Your answers must follow exactly the instructions given. Write in pen, not pencil. You are allowed to make alterations, but see that your work is clear and easy to read.*

1  Write a description of a favourite relative. (About 350 words)

2  'Only when the arms race is halted will there be world peace.' Discuss. (About 350 words)

3  Write a story that ends as follows: 'But there was no reason to blame herself. It was an accident, that's all. A whim of fate, bad luck.' (About 350 words)

4  CITY TRAFFIC GRINDING TO HALT<br>COUNCIL PROMISES ACTION

Write the newspaper report to which these headlines refer. (About 300 words)

5  (See Appendix: Prescribed texts)

# PAPER 3   USE OF ENGLISH   (2 hours)

*Answer all the questions.*
*Your answers must be written in ink in this booklet, using the spaces provided.*

## SECTION A

1   *Fill each of the numbered blanks in the following passage with* **one** *suitable word.*

Success ........................... (1) life depends to a great ........................... (2) on what we mean by success. To some people money is the ........................... (3) real indication of achievement in the modern world. Their estimation of success is ........................... (4) on the state of their bank ........................... (5) and the power that ........................... (6) with it. Their life is devoted to ........................... (7) money and they are at a ........................... (8) to understand people whose ........................... (9) are different from their ........................... (10). There are those, ........................... (11), who consider their lives successful if they are doing what they enjoy doing though it may not bring them any substantial financial ........................... (12). A man who spends his time gardening ........................... (13) consider himself successful if his flowers ........................... (14) and his trees ........................... (15) fruit. Nursing, teaching, running a Youth Club all bring their own ........................... (16) of success to those engaged in them. Success can be found in painting a picture ........................... (17) will ever see, sailing a boat, ........................... (18) the stars, collecting stamps – ........................... (19) anything that involves personal endeavour. The great ........................... (20) is to believe that success is not necessarily public.

2   *Finish each of the following sentences in such a way that it means exactly the same as the sentence printed before it.*

EXAMPLE:   Nobody told us what to expect.

ANSWER:   We *weren't told what to expect.*

a)   It's no use asking John about it.
      There's .................................................................................................................

b)  You can hear a repeat of the programme tomorrow evening.
The programme ........................................................................................

c)  She is a very conscientious worker.
She takes ..............................................................................................

d)  There were no casualties as a result of the accident.
No one .................................................................................................

e)  I have to get a visa before I go to New York next month.
I can't .................................................................................................

f)  My knowledge of Renaissance art is very limited.
I don't .................................................................................................

g)  I couldn't get any meat because all the shops were shut.
None ...................................................................................................

h)  Those children are very disobedient.
Those children never ...........................................................................

3   *Fill each of the blanks with a suitable word or phrase.*

EXAMPLE:   If you're going out, *would you mind* ............... posting this letter for me?

a)  I haven't read the article about health foods. What ...........................
................... say?

b)  Have you ........................................................ mind about your holiday yet?

c)  Although the post has arrived, there's ............................................
you.

d)  I'm afraid you can't ring me, I ........................................... phone.

e)  I thought ........................................... at the door. It must be the
gasman.

f)  That application form looks very complicated, ...................................
................................. a look at it.

g)  There is an old saying 'The higher you climb, ...................................
................................. fall'.

h)  Scones are very expensive now, so I ........................................... make
my own.

4  *For each of the sentences below, write a new sentence* **as similar as possible in meaning to the original sentence,** *but using the word given. This word must* **not be altered** *in any way.*

EXAMPLE:  The idea never occurred to me.
**crossed**

ANSWER:  *The idea never crossed my mind.*

a)  They probably won't get here before ten o'clock.
**unlikely**

b)  My passport expires at the end of August.
**valid**

c)  He is always late for work.
**time**

d)  The Youth Club does not admit members over the age of 18 years.
**membership**

e)  I don't understand all that political jargon.
**beyond**

f)  Did you inherit that old clock from your grandfather?
**leave**

g)  All our trainees have to have a medical test.
**compulsory**

h)  You can't expect to start a new business without experiencing any problems.
**bound**

## SECTION B

5  *Read the following passage, then answer the questions which follow it.*

An increasingly fruitful recreation for passengers on a long motorway drive is 'counting the kestrels', spotting the predatory birds suspended in the air above the embankments.

Hovering kestrels, alert for edible activity below, are the most easily visible signs of
5  a surprising world of wildlife which is flourishing on the fringes of Britain's 2,000 miles of motorways.

Imprisoned between a relentless stream of fast traffic on one side, and chemically cleansed farmland on the other, motorway verges are blossoming as unspoiled nature reserves – a total of some 18,000 acres of them.

10  The law forbids stopping on the motorway other than in an emergency, so human visitors on the verges are rare. There are no farm animals to graze and trample the soft ground, and with no chemical pesticides the soil flourishes organically.

There is even evidence that the turbulence of passing vehicles, combined with oxides of nitrogen emitted in exhaust gases, are richly increasing the levels of nitrogen
15  in vegetation alongside motorways.

As a result there is an abundance of insects, which rely on the nitrogen content of plants for building proteins, and which themselves become a vital link in the food chain which encourages other forms of wildlife to congregate on the motorway edges.

The kestrels are an airborne clue to the growing populations of voles, mice, rabbits,
20  frogs, toads, newts and smaller birds which we pass within a few feet as we travel along the motorways. There are also hedgehogs, foxes and badgers colonising sections of the embankments.

The debris of motorway traffic does not seem to discourage them. On the contrary.

There is no excuse, of course, for travellers polluting the verges with litter. But
25  unsightly, non-biodegradable items such as plastic or glass bottles, soft drink cans and lost car hubcaps have been found by scientists to have been taken over by colonies of ants, nesting birds, voles and mice, and by the same small animals sheltering from the marauding kestrels.

The hard shoulder, designated for breakdown emergencies, is popular territory for
30  crows and hedgehogs foraging for the corpses of insects which impact with, and ricochet off, passing vehicles.

It is not only the animals which are flourishing. Splashes of colour amid the green of motorway embankments in spring and summer betray the wild flowers which are spreading there.

35  Look out for corn poppies appearing beside any newly completed stretch of motorway. Their dormant seeds flourish in newly-turned earth, which was the reason for their abundance in the Flanders fields of wartime France, and in freshly planted British fields before the use of chemical weedkillers became so prevalent in agriculture.

a)  Why are the kestrels 'suspended in the air' (line 2)?

........................................................................................................................................................

b) The signs of wildlife on the motorway verges are described as 'surprising' (line 5). Why is this?

.................................................................................................................................................

c) Explain 'nature reserves' and say why the verges are compared to them (line 9).

.................................................................................................................................................

d) How does the soil manage to flourish 'organically' (line 12)?

.................................................................................................................................................

e) Vegetation grows abundantly near the motorways because of the nitrogen in the soil. How does it get there?

.................................................................................................................................................

f) What does 'themselves' refer to (line 17)?

.................................................................................................................................................

g) Describe the 'food chain' (lines 17–18).

.................................................................................................................................................

h) What is the significance of the presence of the kestrels?

.................................................................................................................................................

i) Explain the 'debris' and say what is good and bad about it (line 23).

.................................................................................................................................................

j) Explain 'hard shoulder' and say why crows and hedgehogs are found there (line 29).

.................................................................................................................................................

k) What does the phrase 'foraging for the corpses' mean (line 30)?

.................................................................................................................................................

l) Why were corn poppies found in the Flanders fields in wartime?

.................................................................................................................................................

m) In 60–80 words summarise the reasons for the growth of wildlife along the motorway verges.

.................................................................................................................................................

.................................................................................................................................................

.................................................................................................................................................

.................................................................................................................................................

.................................................................................................................................................

# PAPER 4  LISTENING COMPREHENSION  (Approx. 30 minutes)

*Further instructions will be given on the recording. Your answers must be written in ink in this booklet, using the spaces provided.*

### FIRST PART

*For question 1, look at the eight instructions for doing the Test Pilot test. Put them in the right order and then write the correct numbers in the boxes. Number 1 has been done for you.*

1 a) label parts

   b) cut paper to size                              | 1 |

   c) let ruler drop unexpectedly

   d) divide the rule into three sections

   e) stick paper down

   f) ask friend to hold hand out

   g) wrap paper around the ruler

   h) mark off 1 cm from the bottom of ruler

*For each of the questions 2–5, put a tick in one of the boxes A, B, C or D.*

2  Brian labels the ruler to

   A  measure its length.            | A |

   B  test his reflexes.             | B |

   C  calculate a reaction.          | C |

   D  estimate its mobility.         | D |

3  From what George says about the test he seems to be

   A  confused by Brian's instructions.   | A |

   B  sceptical about its accuracy.        | B |

   C  interested to see how it works.      | C |

   D  bored by the proceedings.            | D |

4   We get the impression that Brian is something of

    A   a time and motion expert.

    B   an aeronautical specialist.

    C   an amateur scientist.

    D   a lay psychologist.

| |
|---|
| A |
| B |
| C |
| D |

5   It seems a ruler can be used to test someone's reflexes by getting them to

    A   drop it from a height.

    B   catch it in midair.

    C   hold it tightly.

    D   clutch the end of it.

| |
|---|
| A |
| B |
| C |
| D |

## SECOND PART

*For each of the questions 6–8, put a tick in one of the boxes A, B, C or D.*

6   The report states that the miners

    A   have refused to go to the coal board.

    B   are continuing industrial action.

    C   have increased their pay demands.

    D   have contravened Union rules.

| |
|---|
| A |
| B |
| C |
| D |

7   As a result of the trouble at Bankside Colliery

    A   five pickets are in hospital.

    B   three policemen injured the pickets.

    C   several people have been arrested.

    D   the police dismantled the winding gear.

| |
|---|
| A |
| B |
| C |
| D |

8   The authorities state that if the strike continues for more than a fortnight

    A   power stations will be closed.

    B   coal supplies will be halted.

    C   power will be cut off throughout the country.

    D   electricity supplies will be a risk.

| |
|---|
| A |
| B |
| C |
| D |

## THIRD PART

*For questions 9–14 fill in the information about the planned visits. Day One has been done for you. For each of the questions 15–19 put a tick in one of the boxes A, B, C or D.*

### *Orlando Stop and See Holiday*

| | | |
|---|---|---|
| | DAY ONE | Arrive Orlando hotel – afternoon free |
| (9) | DAY TWO | |
| (10) | DAY THREE | |
| (11) | DAY FOUR | |
| (12) | DAY FIVE | |
| (13) | DAY SIX | |
| (14) | DAY SEVEN | |

15  Lyn is going on a

   A   coach trip.

   B   fly – drive holiday.

   C   conducted tour.

   D   two-centre holiday.

| |
|---|
| A |
| B |
| C |
| D |

16  When she visits Sea World, Lyn will find herself in a

   A   wildlife conservation area.

   B   marine-life park.

   C   aquatic sports centre.

   D   safari park.

| |
|---|
| A |
| B |
| C |
| D |

17  At the Kennedy Space Center tourists can

   A   enter a spacecraft.

   B   explore the mysteries of space.

   C   acquire knowledge of space exploration.

   D   communicate with a satellite.

| |
|---|
| A |
| B |
| C |
| D |

18    In order to go on this holiday, Lyn eventually had to

   A    get an overdraft.

   B    work overtime.

   C    borrow from her family.

   D    spend all her savings.

| A |
|---|
| B |
| C |
| D |

19    From the passage, we get the impression that Lyn

   A    is inclined to be irresponsible.

   B    always gets what she wants.

   C    is extravagant by nature.

   D    has an extrovert personality.

| A |
|---|
| B |
| C |
| D |

## FOURTH PART

*Look at the diagram of the stage plot at the beginning of Act 1, Scene 1 and then answer questions 20–22. For questions 20 and 21, tick one of the boxes, A, B, C or D. For question 22, write the answers in the boxes.*

Act 1, Scene 1

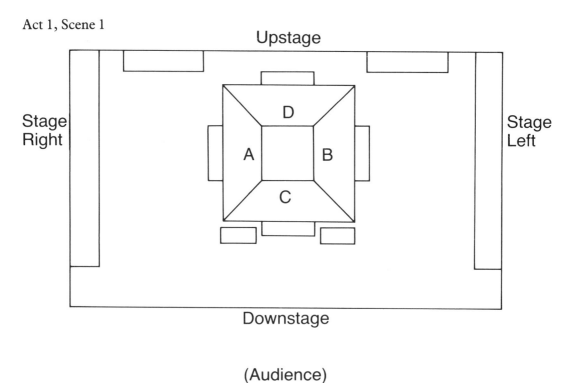

20  Which of the following diagrams shows the stage plot at the beginning of Act 1, Scene 2?

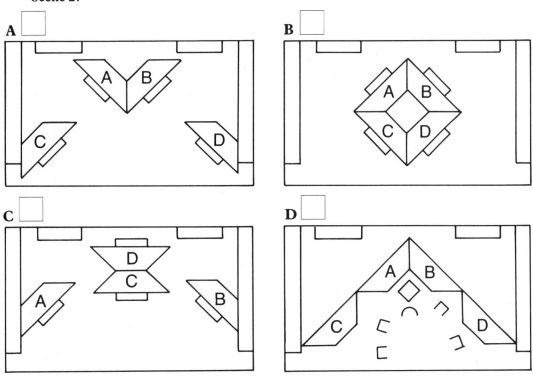

21  Which of these stage plots does the director describe as 'rather tricky'?

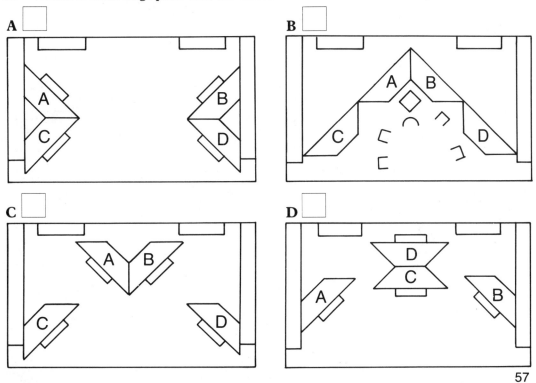

22 This diagram shows the stage plots for the complete opera but they are not in the right order. Write the names of the different acts and scenes in the boxes beside the diagrams. Act 1, Scene 1 and Act 2, Scene 1 have been done for you.

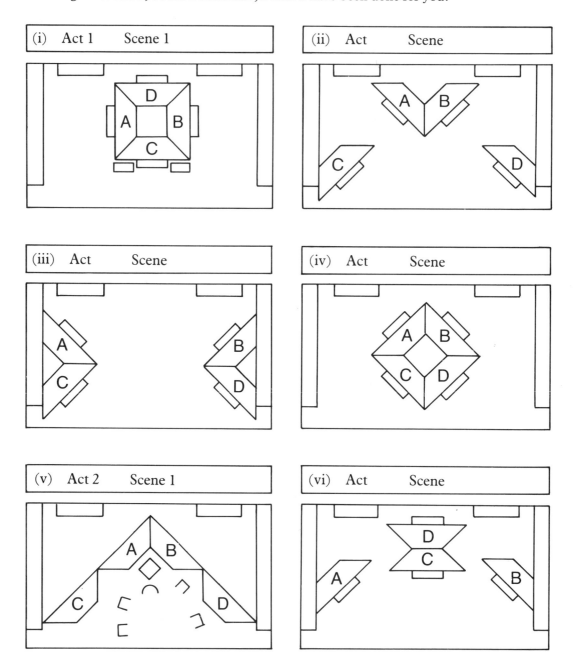

# PAPER 5  INTERVIEW  (Approx. 15 minutes)

*Look at this photograph carefully and be prepared to describe and discuss it.*

a)  Describe the women.
       the event.
       what is happening.

b)  Health and fitness.
    Beauty contests.
    Sport and drugs.

c)  *Study one or more of the following passages and be prepared to answer questions or make comments on the subject matter.*

(i)  Carolyn Cheshire is a judge of international standing of women's body-building contests. In her opinion an aesthetic of female body-building is just beginning to take shape. 'You can only get detail by long-term training. It's no good having muscles which look as though they have been thrown on.' And she said that although she had heard rumours of drug use in the past, drug-testing will, for the first time, be mandatory in next year's world championships.

(ii) Drug scandals in American sport seem never-ending, and they are always followed by a row about the need for compulsory drug-testing. . . The revelation that seven members of the New England Patriots were secretly treated for cocaine or marijuana addiction during the season came immediately after the team's overwhelming defeat in the Super Bowl. Fans were assured the players had been 'clean' for weeks before the big game, and the whole team volunteered to submit to a drug-testing programme next season.

(iii) A trimming toy, whether it's a cycle machine or a more modest system of ropes with weights, should help you to improve the all-round efficiency of your body, and it should improve the suppleness, the strength and the stamina. That means progressive exercising; it means improving the efficiency of your heart and lungs and exercising your muscles to extend their maximum range.

d) General discussion:

*Study the photographs and advice given about the two different ways of exercising and be prepared to give your opinion on their relative merits.*

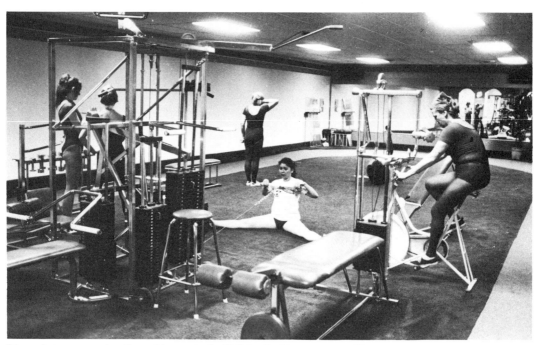

**Pinpoint concentration.** Aim eyeballs. Grit teeth. Narrow eyes. Plant feet. Square shoulders. Aim eyeballs. Flex toes. Grunt/growl/groan. Grasp bar. Aim eyeballs. Stamp feet. Row oars. Catch sandbag. S-t-r-e-t-c-h. Aim eyeballs. Pump arms. Gasp breath. Spread toes. Tighten grip. Whiten knuckles. Lash out. Aim eyeballs. Brain punchbag. Skip rope. Push/pull/push. Shove harder. Gasp in. Tilt jaw. Shrug shoulders. Aim eyeballs. Aim eyeballs. Aim eyeballs.
Note: concentrate intensely seeing nothing in front of you – eyeballs focussed on only one target: boosting muscles to utmost potential you desire.

- Practise the asanas on an empty stomach, or at least two hours after a meal.

- Always try to synchronise your breathing with your movements.

- Yoga demands that the attention of the mind is fixed on every movement performed.

- When you do an exercise, always work slowly; not with speed or jerkiness. A Yoga movement must be slow, supple and gentle.

- Never forget (absolutely never) that a Yoga which hurts is a Yoga badly performed. The absence of pain is a proof of perfection.

- Remember that Yoga demands a complete abolition of the spirit of competition.


*and/or*

e)    Short talk:

*Single candidate*
Describe any form of exercise you have ever done and how you felt about it.

*Group*
Describe and compare your experiences of exercising.

f)    (See Appendix: Prescribed texts)

# Test Four

## PAPER 1  READING COMPREHENSION  (1 hour)

*Answer all questions. Indicate your choice of answer in every case* **on the separate answer
sheet** *already given out, which should show your name and examination index number.
Follow carefully the instructions about how to record your answers. Give* **one answer only** *to
each question. Marks will not be deducted for wrong answers: your total score on this test will be
the number of correct answers you give.*

### SECTION A

*In this section you must choose the word or phrase which best completes each sentence.* **On your
answer sheet** *indicate the letter A, B, C or D against the number of each item 1 to 25 for the
word or phrase you choose.*

1   The Presiding Officer will give you a ................. paper at the polling station.
    A canvassing    B election    C voting    D ballot

2   He was an illegal immigrant and was ................. within the year.
    A despatched    B exported    C deported    D exiled

3   These cameras are designed for ................. who want to do more than just take snaps.
    A them    B these    C those    D they

4   She felt the situation had got ................. and there was no way she could control it.
    A out of hand    B out of line    C out of place    D out of step

5   Some of the best golf ................. are to be found in Scotland.
    A tracks    B pitches    C courses    D courts

6   The large canoes made in the Gilbert Islands are ................. by 30,000 metres of string
    made from coconut husks.
    A held up    B held together    C held off    D held in

7   In the examination you may be asked for comments on various ................. of a topic.
    A qualities    B aspects    C features    D angles

8   She entered the competition and waited for the results ................. .
    A out of breath    B under her breath    C with bated breath    D in the same
    breath

9   The roar of the MGM lion ................. the beginning of their films.
    A renounces    B pronounces    C denounces    D announces

10  I'll say goodbye now ................. I don't see you again.
    A in case    B unless    C even if    D allowing for

62

11  In one of Schubert's quintets, the first violin ................. a quail, which was thought to be a holy bird.
A  resembles     B  reflects     C  represents     D  reproduces

12  It is ................. impossible to find a good educational computer program.
A  barely     B  merely     C  hardly     D  nearly

13  At the festival you can hear music ................. over a system of twenty loudspeakers.
A  reproduced     B  relayed     C  realised     D  propelled

14  Many people complain of the rapid ................. of modern life.
A  rate     B  gait     C  pace     D  march

15  If your cat often has to stay indoors, then provide a ................. tray for it.
A  waste     B  litter     C  rubbish     D  garbage

16  Traditionally, a business deal was ................. by a handshake.
A  sealed     B  conceded     C  sanctioned     D  carried

17  They were doubtful whether the relationship would succeed but decided to ................. .
A  work it out     B  get it together     C  give it a try     D  put it in hand

18  Tim worked so hard for the exam that it was ................. that he passed with distinction.
A  inevitable     B  irrevocable     C  inconceivable     D  irrefutable

19  Take out a Householder's Insurance Policy and you can ................. the rewards of regular saving.
A  gain     B  reap     C  draw     D  earn

20  The idea for a new video game slowly began to ................. in his mind.
A  draw breath     B  turn out     C  come about     D  take shape

21  I'm not ................. interested in grammar as in learning new vocabulary.
A  as much     B  even so     C  very much     D  nearly so

22  With a word ................. you can produce a document much faster than with a typewriter.
A  processor     B  computer     C  printer     D  copier

23  Due to the extreme weather conditions the mountain road was ................. .
A  impossible     B  inoperable     C  impassable     D  impregnable

24  All the theatre seats were sold and there was standing ................. only.
A  place     B  area     C  space     D  room

25  She'll have to ................. herself together if she wants to keep her job.
A  take     B  put     C  draw     D  pull

## SECTION B

*In this section you will find after each of the passages a number of questions or unfinished statements about the passage, each with four suggested answers or ways of finishing. You must choose the one which you think fits best according to the passage.* **On your answer sheet** *indicate the letter A, B, C or D against the number of each item 26 to 40 for the answer you choose. Give* **one answer only** *to each question. Read each passage right through before choosing your answers.*

## FIRST PASSAGE

After a while I grew tired of the confusion and disturbance of the town. There were several bars open, one offered a *cocktail feminino* which I was curious to know more about. Instead I decided to remain sober and drove out of town and up to the Paso de Cortes, the high pass by which the conquistadores had broken through the Aztec defences. These are the foothills of the Sierra Madre Oriental and on a clear day the view from Amecameca is dominated by the two volcanoes, Popocatepetl and Ixtaccihuatl. This was not a clear day. The heat haze pressed down beneath a layer of high cloud which hid the mountain peaks. The road started to climb through thick woodland. Indian women stood in some of the clearings, tending fires. They held out the tortillas they had been cooking, hoping for a sale. Their horses were tethered nearby; presumably they were on the last stage of their journey to the fair. They would be in town by nightfall, in time for the procession.

As I emerged from the woods, the clouds, which had hidden Popocatepetl for several weeks, suddenly lifted and the peak stood distinct in the cold blue air. The peak was covered in snow and from the tip of this arose a thin plume of smoke. Below the ring of snow the volcanic slopes were rumpled into pleats of soft brown and grey. Not a tree or a blade of grass could be seen on those slopes.

The Aztecs believed that Popocatepetl was a former king and that Ixtaccihuatl, 'The Sleeping Woman' was his faithful wife who accompanied him in death. I wondered what Cortes would have thought of all this beauty as he was guided between the volcanoes and knew that the guardian saints of the Aztecs were nothing more than volcanoes. It was as deserted now on the windy brown plateau as it was on the day he passed. Cortes is not honoured in Mexico – there are only two statues to him in the entire country – but on the Paso de Cortes a small bas-relief has been set into a stone. This shows him advancing, mounted on an armoured horse, a crowd of men around him and the Indian interpreter, Princess Marina, who bore his son, showing him the way. Without Marina, the Spanish could never have left the coast. They numbered only five hundred, but their arrival had been prophesied in the Aztec religion, of which, with Marina's help, they were able to take advantage and save themselves from Montezuma's sacrificial altars.

In truth Cortes needs no monuments in Mexico; the whole country is a result of his reckless adventure. Every church in Mexico is his monument, just as much as the medieval suits of armour which were being sold to the children in the town below the pass. A chill wind from the volcano started to blow and I returned to the warmth of the forest and the mist.

26 The writer decided to leave the town because

 A there was too much confusion in the bars.

 B he was wary of the effects of cocktails.

 C he didn't want to become an alcoholic.

 D only one of the bars served cocktails.

27 The foothills of the mountains were

 A wreathed in mists.

 B inhabited by Indians.

 C covered in forest.

 D blanketed in snow.

28 The legends of the Aztec suggest that

 A neither of the volcanoes had ever erupted.

 B one of their kings had died in a volcano.

 C the wife of the king had been sacrificed.

 D the Indians worshipped the volcanoes.

29 Why was Cortes, the Spanish general, able to conquer the Aztecs?

 A His army outnumbered the Indians.

 B He embraced the Aztec religion.

 C The Indians were very superstitious.

 D He was married to an Aztec princess.

30 Cortes completely reshaped Mexico by

 A introducing Christianity.

 B destroying all Aztec monuments.

 C instigating armoured warfare.

 D influencing the children.

## SECOND PASSAGE

Anyone interested in visiting one of the most futuristic observatories in the world should begin by heading for Gourdon, in southern France, and from there start to climb up into the French Alps. As one approaches the 1,200 metre mark, he will see, at the very edge of the cliff above, the tip of the dome that encloses one of the world's most powerful astronomical instruments, a 200-inch Schmidt telescope. Climbing higher, the visitor will see a dozen other structures scattered across the plateau. Some are strangly shaped – like two objects that resemble giant inverted mushrooms and one building complex that resembles a large, concrete molehill. This is the Calern Observatory. It is a bold plan to gather on one site a collection of some of the latest high-technology instruments in astrometry. Astrometry concerns itself with the direct measurement of dimensions in the universe. This includes not only the positions in the sky of stars and planets but also the measurement of their diameters and of astronomical time. Astronomers have recently begun to use lasers to determine the distances to the satellites and to the moon.

Astrometry is the most fundamental part of astronomy. The star catalogues that other astronomers use to find targets and that navigators use to fix their locations on Earth are made possible by astrometry. So are the tables that keep track of the paths of the sun, moon and planets through the star field. Calculations of eclipses, sunrise and sunset, phases of the moon, and the direction of the true north are all astrometrically based. The Calern Observatory hopes to perfect such products.

31  What does the Calern Observatory consist of?

A   A dome-shaped building surrounded by other structures.

B   Various odd-shaped buildings scattered throughout the French Alps.

C   A domed building at the edge of a plateau near a dozen other structures.

D   A number of buildings on a plateau with a domed-shaped structure lower in the Alps.

32  Astrometry enables astronomers to

A   redefine astronomical time.

B   draw maps of the universe.

C   measure the density of satellites.

D   calculate the position of planets.

33    To find their way navigators

   A    use laser beams.

   B    consult star catalogues.

   C    fix their locations by the planets.

   D    follow the sun and moon paths.

34    The importance of the Calern Observatory is its

   A    unique position in the French Alps.

   B    collection of high-tech instruments.

   C    development and research facilities.

   D    involvement in space exploration.

## THIRD PASSAGE

*Extract 1*
One of the most striking features of any cat is its beautiful coat. Yet, from the cat's point of view, the important thing about the coat and the skin beneath it is not their appearance but their role in protecting the cat and in helping to maintain its bodily equilibrium. They form a barrier between the outside world and the rest of the cat's body, preventing excessive water loss from the tissues and providing protection against physical injuries, heat and cold, harmful chemicals and excessive sunlight, as well as the invasion of germs.

*Extract 2*
SAGITTARIUS (November 23 – December 20): a dreamy cat with the speed of a horse but the brain of a bird. This unsettling combination usually makes him as uncomfortable as he makes you. Not good in town – a delapidated castle or old manor house keeps him happiest. Best owners: Sagittarius, Leo, but never Cancer.

*Extract 3*
Yes, a pair of cats. Siamese by preference; for they are certainly the most 'human' of all the race of cats. Also the strangest, and, if not the most beautiful, certainly the most striking and fantastic. For what disquieting pale plue eyes stare out from the black velvet masks of their faces! Snow-white at birth, their bodies gradually darken to a rich mulatto colour. . . And what strange voices they have! Sometimes like the complaining of small children; sometimes like the noise of lambs; sometimes like the agonized and furious howling of lost souls. Compared with these fantastic creatures, other cats, however beautiful and engaging, are apt to seem a little insipid.

*Extract 4*
cat [kæt] *n*. **1.**    small, domesticated fur-covered animal often kept as a pet, to catch mice, etc.; any animal of the group that includes cats, tigers, lions, panthers and leopards.

35  What is the importance of the cat's coat in extract 1?

    A   It helps fight off harmful infections.

    B   It forms a defence system.

    C   It provides an attractive covering.

    D   It helps the cat keep its balance.

36  Sagittarian cats, referred to in extract 2, are likely to

    A   live happily with old people.

    B   be mentally unbalanced.

    C   feel uncomfortable with humans.

    D   be rather simple-minded.

37  In extract 3, a Siamese cat's pale blue eyes are said to be 'disquieting' because they

    A   provide a colour contrast to the fur.

    B   can outstare human beings.

    C   change colour as the cat ages.

    D   look almost like human eyes.

38  'kæt' in extract 4 is probably

    A   cat in a foreign language.

    B   an old English spelling.

    C   cat spelt phonetically.

    D   the old English pronunciation.

39  How are cats considered differently in extract 4 compared with 1, 2 and 3?

    A   They are thought of as pets.

    B   They are described precisely.

    C   They are considered domesticated.

    D   They are equated with wild animals.

40  Compared with extract 1, the description of cats in extract 3 is

    A   more personal.

    B   less exact.

    C   rather vague.

    D   over-sentimental.

## PAPER 2   COMPOSITION   (2 hours)

*Write **two only** of the following composition exercises. Your answers must follow exactly the instructions given. Write in pen, not pencil. You are allowed to make alterations, but see that your work is clear and easy to read.*

1   Imagine you are a teacher in a large school. Write a descriptive account of a working day. (About 350 words)

2   'English is the most important international language.' Discuss. (About 350 words)

3   You have to spend the weekend alone in the country without any transport. Choose three things to take with you and explain why you have chosen them. (About 350 words)

4   Below are the notes you have on 'Starting Your Own Business'. From them, write the speech you will make to the local business college. (About 350 words)

Starting your own business
(possibilities)

① Buy out own employer

② Strike out on own within own trade or profession

③ Acquire existing business

④ Start from scratch

⑤ Buy franchise
(action)
See bank manager

5   (See Appendix: Prescribed texts)

# PAPER 3  USE OF ENGLISH  (2 hours)

*Answer* **all** *the questions.*
*Your answers must be written in ink in this booklet, using the spaces provided.*

## SECTION A

1  *Fill each of the numbered blanks in the following passage with* **one** *suitable word.*

Teachers have long been ............................ (1) of the wide gap between the ............................ (2) of children's work in ............................ (3) fields as painting and writing and their efforts in mathematics. In the past two decades we have seen the gradual ............................ (4) of mathematical work ............................ (5) on personal discovery and understanding. Teachers can now provide ............................ (6) of children's ability to ............................ (7) significant and personal discoveries in maths ............................ (8) has long been the tradition in ............................ (9) fields of curriculum experience. ............................ (10) last, maths is becoming closely ............................ (11) with an understanding of children and ............................ (12) they learn. Listening to children discussing their work ............................ (13) reveals that they are ............................ (14) more involved in maths than the traditional analysis of 'problem work' ever ............................ (15). Their processes do not ............................ (16) the neat forms suggested by arithmetic books. Children solve ............................ (17) in changeable rhythmical patterns. They bring to the work their ............................ (18) associations and experience. They have 'lucky numbers', 'my house number' and even 'my mum's age'; these associations are often ............................ (19) enough to swamp the teacher's ............................ (20) to a mathematical problem.

2  *Finish each of the following sentences in such a way that it means exactly the same as the sentence printed before it.*

> EXAMPLE:  'Unless you improve your time-keeping, I'll sack you.'
>
> ANSWER:  'If *you don't improve your time-keeping, I'll sack you.'*

a)  In spite of bad weather, everyone enjoyed the fair.
    Although .................................................................................................................

b)  She is a more imaginative chess player than her sister.
    She plays ............................................................................................................

c)  'You mustn't touch the rocker switch' the supervisor told the men.
    The supervisor instructed ..............................................................................

d)  Never underestimate the importance of a good family life.
    The importance ................................................................................................

e)  The punch was so hard that it broke the boxer's nose.
    It was ..................................................................................................................

f)  I closed the door and a shot rang out.
    Hardly .................................................................................................................

g)  Brewers use hops and malt to make beer.
    Beer .....................................................................................................................

h)  I dislike typing articles more than I dislike writing them.
    It is not so much ..............................................................................................

3  *Fill each of the blanks with a suitable word or phrase.*

> EXAMPLE:  Where *can I post* this letter? In the pillar box over there.

a)  I've got a terrible headache, I ................................................................ aspirin.

b)  If ........................................................................ , I wouldn't have done it.

c)  Although I'd met him before, I ............................................................ name.

d)  I would sooner ........................................................ than the theatre.

e)  Instead of grumbling, why ........................................................ something?

f)  Even after explaining it to her for the umpteenth time, I ...........................
    ................... understand.

4 *For each of the sentences below, write a new sentence* **as similar as possible in meaning to the original sentence,** *but using the word given. This word must* **not be altered** *in any way.*

> EXAMPLE: The large number of guests at his party was evidence of his popularity.
> **popular**

> ANSWER: *The large number of guests at his party showed how popular he was.*

a) Although he is very old, he still walks round the park every day.
**despite**

.................................................................................................................................

b) I had no idea you came from Brazil.
**know**

.................................................................................................................................

c) It's true he's a brilliant scientist, but otherwise he's rather stupid.
**although**

.................................................................................................................................

d) I was surprised to see how much food she ate.
**never**

.................................................................................................................................

e) Eventually, he gave in to pressure from the others.
**end**

.................................................................................................................................

f) Can you prove your allegations?
**proof**

.................................................................................................................................

g) Simon was practically illiterate.
**hardly**

.................................................................................................................................

h) He failed to understand her motives.
**incomprehensible**

.................................................................................................................................

## SECTION B

5   *Read the following passage, and then answer the questions that follow it.*

The idea of listing hated books does not have an immediate appeal. Why hate a piece of creation even if it is at the bottom end of one's own appreciation scale? Why not just put that particular book aside and let its contents remain secure within their covers, disliked certainly – but hated?

5      I think the nearest I have come to loathing is with textbooks, and for two reasons: they were compulsory reading, and they frequently succeeded in turning all the gold of this world into lead. I did not, and I do not, see why they had to be so dull, and I certainly resented them for it. They, above all else, represented the educational system of sham pearls being cast before real swine. They took the wondrous facts and

10   transformed these into turgid lists, interspersed with pea-soup prose and dismal diagram. It was as if no excitement or joy should be set before a student, in case it might stimulate him or her into original thought, or happiness. Learning from a dreary text was proof both of application and of spirit. To spare this form of rod was to spoil the child.

15      They say that textbooks for today's pupils are better, just as they say that the schools are better. I hope they are, and that some of the more awful texts have been swept aside. I do not know which was the worst, as of course I encountered them at different ages and when differently equipped to object to them; but I think the largest seal of disapproval should be awarded to those enforced upon the older, more discriminating

20   but still fettered student, such as those in their middle teens. I was then subjected to *Intermediate Physics* and *Higher School Inorganic Chemistry*, but I think abysmal pride of place should go to *The Invertebrata*.

Why did I dislike it so much? Well, it changed the wonder of the invertebrate world into indigestible latinised tedium. How's this for openers as its first sentence? 'The

25   invertebrata have long since ceased to constitute one of the primary divisions in the scientific classification of the Animal Kingdom.' What was the book's title again, and how's that for an immediate rebuff? However it never lets up: 'This type is said to possess the caridoid facies.', 'The Protozoa are sundered from the rest of the Animal Kingdom. . .', 'Of the appendages or limbs of the crustacea, the first, or atennule, is a

30   structure *sui generis*. . .'. Coupled with such porridge were occasional, but always nasty, little drawings that also sought to uninspire. It was a book to be resented, deeply, for its lack of warmth, of life, of feeling, but the fact that it was compulsory reading did, I suppose, depress one's considerable dislike into a form of hatred. I have certainly not enjoyed collecting it from the library to refresh my memory of its

35   particular depths, a nadir that so many others have tried to emulate but few, happily, have achieved so well.

a)   What is referred to in the phrase 'piece of creation' (lines 1–2)?

.........................................................................................................................................................................

b) Explain the meaning of 'loathing' (line 5).

.............................................................................................................

c) What does the writer mean by 'turning all the gold of the world into lead' (lines 6–7)?

.............................................................................................................

d) What does 'it' refer to (line 8)?

.............................................................................................................

e) 'They' at the beginning of line 8 refers to

.............................................................................................................

f) What is meant by 'sham pearls' (line 9)?

.............................................................................................................

g) Who are the 'real swine' (line 9)?

.............................................................................................................

h) What does the writer resent happening to the 'wondrous facts' (line 9)?

.............................................................................................................

i) What is meant by the phrase 'pea-soup prose' (line 10)?

.............................................................................................................

j) What does the writer imply was the purpose of uninteresting texts?

.............................................................................................................

k) What does 'this form of rod' refer to (line 13)?

.............................................................................................................

l) How was the writer 'differently equipped' to deal with textbooks at different ages (line 18)?

.............................................................................................................

m) In a paragraph of 60–80 words summarise the writer's attitide towards, and feelings about, textbooks.

.............................................................................................................

.............................................................................................................

.............................................................................................................

.............................................................................................................

.............................................................................................................

# PAPER 4  LISTENING COMPREHENSION  (Approx. 30 minutes)

*Further instructions will be given on the recording. Your answers must be written in ink in this booklet, using the spaces provided.*

## FIRST PART

*For questions 1–6, fill in the correct answer. For question 7 write the answers in the boxes.*

| | | |
|---|---|---|
| Name of radio station | 1 | |
| Number of listeners | 2 | |
| Radio station's reason for the hunt | 3 | |
| Date of the acorn hunt | 4 | |
| Main place for the acorn hunt | 5 | |
| Number of children's prizes | 6 | |

7   The drawings below show the damage done to acorns by animals and birds. Write the name of the animal or bird in the box beside each drawing.

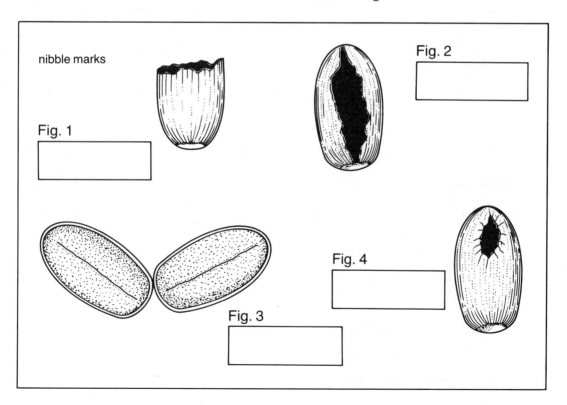

nibble marks

Fig. 1

Fig. 2

Fig. 3

Fig. 4

## SECOND PART

*For questions 8–15, tick whether you think the statements are true or false.*

| | True | False |
|---|---|---|

8    Hilary works for a dance company called 'Send a Song'.

9    She often has a job as a tap-dancing gorilla.

10   When performing as a gorilla, Hilary particularly likes being boisterous.

11   According to Hilary, many people are offended when presented by a singing telegram.

12   Hilary started working for 'Send a Song' because she is a trained dancer.

13   Many people are prepared to pay £20 to embarrass their friends.

14   The biggest problem for Hilary is having to wear costumes underneath each other.

15   The policy of the 'Send a Song' company is to write an individual song for each telegram.

## THIRD PART

*For questions 16–19, tick* **one** *of the boxes A, B, C or D.*

16   The woman invites the man to

    A    take part in a demonstration.

    B    sign a declaration.

    C    support local action.

    D    join a protest group.

| |
|---|
| A |
| B |
| C |
| D |

17   The closure of the swimming pool will result in

    A    a lack of any community activity.

    B    unnecessary inconvenience to local residents.

    C    the necessity for an increase in local transport.

    D    an increase in children's accidents.

| |
|---|
| A |
| B |
| C |
| D |

18  The interviewer appears to be concerned about

　　A  the good of the community.

　　B  child development.

　　C  public transport.

　　D  community relations.

| |
|---|
| A |
| B |
| C |
| D |

19  From the man's response we understand that he

　　A  dislikes children.

　　B  is antisocial.

　　C  couldn't care less.

　　D  prefers his own company.

| |
|---|
| A |
| B |
| C |
| D |

## FOURTH PART

*For each of the questions 20–22, put a tick in one of the boxes A, B, C or D.*

20  This advice comes from a

　　A  breakfast cereal packet.

　　B  TV commercial.

　　C  health clinic leaflet.

　　D  talk on diet on the radio.

| |
|---|
| A |
| B |
| C |
| D |

21  The man interviewing the woman is very

　　A  provoking.

　　B  sympathetic.

　　C  officious.

　　D  persuasive.

| |
|---|
| A |
| B |
| C |
| D |

22  From what she says the woman appears to

　　A  encourage hardiness in her children.

　　B  be a long-suffering mother.

　　C  behave as a responsible person.

　　D  over-protect her children.

| |
|---|
| A |
| B |
| C |
| D |

# PAPER 5 INTERVIEW (Approx. 15 minutes)

*Look at this photograph carefully and be prepared to describe and discuss it.*

a) Describe the men.
            the car.
            what has probably happened.

b) Dangerous jobs.
  Accidents.
  Vandalism.

c) *Study one or more of the following passages and be prepared to answer questions or make comments on the subject matter.*

   (i) Fires in the home start in many ways and spread quickly. If you discover a fire in your home which cannot be extinguished immediately and safely, get everyone out of the room where the fire is and close the door in order to confine the spread of fire and smoke. See everyone gets out of the house. Call the fire brigade.

(ii) With effect from 1 April 1986, responsibility for running London's Fire Services and Civil Defence was transferred to the new London Fire and Civil Defence Authority. The London Fire Brigade was reorganised into a five Area Command Structure (previously 11 divisions) which coincided with Borough boundaries. This should enhance the economic, effective and efficient use of the services and increase accountability of the Authority at local level.

(iii) 'I woke up and found the room full of smoke', so said Mrs Ward, interviewed after being rescued from her top floor flat on Friday night. 'I felt really scared as I could hardly breathe with all that smoke. But I managed to get a bedcover round my mouth and nose and stumble into the next room to the phone. The firemen were wonderful, they arrived five minutes later and had me out in no time,' she continued. 'It's certainly a warning to me not to sleep with my electric blanket on.' The fire had been caused by a wire in the blanket overheating and starting the bedclothes smouldering.

d) General discussion:

*Study the leaflet about safety in the home and comment taking the themes listed into consideration.*

# IT'S EASY TO USE ELECTRIC APPLIANCES SAFELY TOO

**Look for the BEAB Mark of Safety on everything you buy.** It's the sign of the British Electrotechnical Approvals Board, awarded only to appliance models that pass rigorous tests for safe construction and operation. Beware of back-street 'bargains'. If they don't bear the BEAB mark, they're not worth the risk. Steer clear of buying appliances secondhand too.

**Keep appliances and flexes in good order.** Have any appliance faults remedied straight away, and major appliances serviced regularly, by a qualified technician. Never let a flex touch hot parts of a fire, toaster, cooker, iron, etc. Replace immediately if damaged.

**Heating. Radiant fires.** Every radiant fire should have a permanent safety guard. Where there are children, an adequate fireguard *must* also be fixed in front of it. Radiant fires in small rooms *must* be fixed high on the wall, at least three feet from any furniture, curtains or doors (open or closed). Always switch off at the wall socket, unplug and let cool before cleaning.

**Convectors.** Never drape anything over a convector (or storage heater). Airing cupboard heaters *must* be shielded against falling clothes, and should have an overheat cut-out and indicator lamp.

**Storage heaters.** Follow maker's instructions for positioning against walls. Keep heaters at least three inches clear of curtains and furniture. Never obstruct air grilles.

**Fan heaters.** Never cover or obstruct air grilles.

**Time switches.** Take special care with time-switched heaters. Make sure they are well clear of curtains, furnishings, etc., at all times.
Time switches and delay controls must never be fitted to radiant fires.

**Lighting.** Buy light fittings from a reputable dealer and take his advice about safety. Switch off before changing light bulbs, and let them cool before removing. Do not exceed the maximum wattage recommended on shades and fittings to avoid the risk of fire.

**Kitchen.** Never handle plugs, switches or any electric appliance with wet hands. Switch off and unplug all appliances before cleaning and make sure they are thoroughly dry before use. Do not allow flexes to overhang work surfaces.

Themes:   Relative cost of ensuring that electrical appliances are safe.
Advantages of regular inspection.
Comparative advice given in your own country.
Other areas of home safety not mentioned in the leaflet.

*and/or*

e)   Short talk:

Describe any accident in the home you have experienced and explain the cause. Say what future precautions should be taken to avoid the same situation occurring. (Compare your experiences with other members of the group.)

f)   (See Appendix: Prescribed texts)

# Test Five

## PAPER 1   READING COMPREHENSION   (1 hour)

*Answer all questions. Indicate your choice of answer on the **separate answer sheet** already given out, which should show your name and examination index number.*
*Follow carefully the instructions about how to record your answers. Give **one answer only** to each question. Marks will not be deducted for wrong answers: your total score on this test will be the number of correct answers you give.*

### SECTION A

*In this section you must choose the word or phrase which best completes each sentence. **On your answer sheet** indicate the letter A, B, C or D against the number of each item 1 to 25 for the word or phrase you choose.*

1   I can't do a thing right today. I'm all ................. .
    A  up the creek      B  fingers and thumbs      C  out of line      D  at cross purposes

2   Because he had no money to pay his debts, he was finally declared ................. .
    A  bankrupt      B  indebted      C  insolvent      D  destitute

3   She left her job on the newspaper and became a ................. journalist.
    A  voluntary      B  freelance      C  itinerant      D  casual

4   Exercise tends to ................. the effects of old age.
    A  offset      B  waylay      C  set back      D  run down

5   The students ................. ever use the language laboratories.
    A  almost      B  practically      C  hardly      D  nearly

6   The workers complained that they were kept ................. about the future of the company.
    A  in the dark      B  in the shade      in the background      D  in purdah

7   I haven't the slightest idea of what I ................. to do in this situation.
    A  could      B  ought      C  would      D  should

8   There was strong government ................. to the workers' demand for a 32 hour week.
    A  dissociation      B  contention      C  dissension      D  opposition

9   Holiday-makers had to ................. with strong winds and heavy rain.
    A  combat      B  contend      C  strive      D  resist

10   'I can read you like ................. ,' she said.
    A  a blank page      B  a closed chapter      C  an open book      D  the spoken word

11   The young man was told to ................. his ideas or leave the agency.
     A conform     B inform     C reform     D deform

12   The actor ................. a famous politician's voice on the radio.
     A took off     B took in     C took down     D took up

13   There's an old saying which states 'you can't make an omelette without ................. '.
     A cracking shells     B whipping whites     C breaking eggs     D separating yolks

14   The 10.50 train arrived on time, ................. the 11.10 was late as usual.
     A wherein     B whereas     C wherefore     D whereat

15   The travel agency offered a £5 ................. for every £50 spent on a holiday booked
     through them.
     A receipt     B docket     C coupon     D voucher

16   The book was the ................. of many years' teaching experience.
     A effect     B product     C outcome     D issue

17   She agreed to read and be ................. by the conditions set out on the back of the leaflet.
     A confined     B bound     C limited     D restricted

18   They didn't really fall out but just ................. from each other.
     A edged away     B got away     C wandered away     D drifted away

19   Wolves are said to howl at the moon when it is ................. .
     A full     B round     C whole     D complete

20   ................. , she felt she had made a good impression on the chairman.
     A In the long run     B All in all     C To crown it all     D All the way

21   The weather looked very doubtful as a ................. of clouds built up in the sky.
     A bank     B edge     C ridge     D ledge

22   During the 1920s, potatoes were the ................. diet of the Irish people.
     A majority     B bulk     C staple     D sum

23   Pure silk has a ................. all of its own.
     A polish     B lustre     C gloss     D sheen

24   Hire charges for video tapes are ................. on an overnight basis.
     A valuated     B assessed     C estimated     D calculated

25   Not wishing to give offence, he approached the subject rather ................. .
     A demurely     B gingerly     C diligently     D wistfully

## SECTION B

*In this section you will find after each of the passages a number of questions or unfinished statements about the passage, each with four suggested answers or ways of finishing. You must choose the one you think fits best according to the passage.* **On your answer sheet** *indicate the letter A, B, C or D against the number of each item 26 to 40 for the answer you choose. Give* **one answer only** *to each question. Read each passage right through before choosing your answers.*

## FIRST PASSAGE

The teacher of reading is involved, whether this is consciously realised or not, in the development of a literate society. And every teacher, therefore, needs to determine what level of literacy is demanded by society, what role he or she should take in achieving the desired standard of literacy, and what the implications of literacy are in a world context.

The Unesco report presents a world view of literacy. Too often we limit our thoughts to the relatively small proportion of illiterates in our own country and fail to see it in its international context.

The problems facing developing nations are also facing industrialised nations. Literacy, as the report points out, is 'inextricably intertwined with other aspects of national development . . . (and) . . . national development as a whole is bound up with the world context'. Literacy is not a by-product of social and economical development – it is a component of that development. Literacy can help people to function more effectively in a changing environment and ideally will enable the individual to change the environment so that it functions more effectively.

Literacy programmes instituted in different countries have taken and are taking different approaches to the problem: for example the involvement of voluntary non-governmental organisations, which underlines the importance of seeing literacy not as a condition imposed on people but as a consequence of active participation within society. People can learn from the attempts of other countries to provide an adequate 'literacy environment'.

Who are the 'illiterates' and how do we define them? At what point do we decide that illiteracy ends and literacy begins? Robert Hillerich addresses these questions. An illiterate, he finds, 'may mean anything from one who has *no* formal schooling to one who has attended four years or less, to one who is unable to read or write at the level necessary to perform successfully in his social position.' Literacy, he points out, is not something one either has or has not got: 'Any definition of literacy must recognise this quality as a continuum, representing all degrees of development.'

An educational definition – i.e. in terms of grades completed or skills mastered – is shown to be inadequate in that educationally defined mastery may bear only minimal relation to the language proficiency needed in coping with environmental demands. From a sociological/economic viewpoint the literacy needs of individuals vary greatly, and any definition must recognise the needs of the individual to engage effectively and to act with responsible participation.

Such a broadened definition excludes assessment based on a 'reading-level type'; assessment must, rather, be flexible to fit both purpose and population.

26 Part of the teacher of reading's involvement in the development of a literate society is through

    A   ascertaining their society's literacy standard.

    B   determining a level of literacy for their society.

    C   deciding on a world standard of literacy.

    D   achieving a desired role for teaching literacy.

27 What problems are facing both developing and industrial nations?

    A   How to achieve literacy in their own countries.

    B   How the environment can be changed to suit the people.

    C   What methods of producing social and economical development can be found.

    D   Which ways of encouraging literacy as part of national development are possible.

28 What importance do the voluntary non-governmental organisations have in literacy programmes?

    A   They demonstrate how literacy changes society.

    B   They show that literacy is often imposed on people.

    C   They present conditions in which people can become literate.

    D   They enable people to take part in international literacy schemes.

29 'Illiterates' according to Hillerich, are best defined as people who

    A   cannot read or write at all.

    B   only have a primary education.

    C   read and write inadequately for their needs.

    D   have no education at all.

30 Why is a 'reading-level type' of assessment inadequate to define literacy?

    A   It ignores other social factors in society.

    B   Educational needs are not taken into account.

    C   Individual involvement in society is not considered.

    D   No account is taken of the importance of language in society.

## SECOND PASSAGE

Bottles of retsina, trays of baklava cakes and thousands of letters clutter the tiny radio studio. All have been sent from well-wishers to London Greek Radio, one of about 80 unlicensed radio stations now filling the airwaves of Britain.

London Greek Radio started broadcasting Greek music, plays, live church services and children's stories nearly eighteen months ago. Its North London transmitters were confiscated many times during its early days, but for the last thirteen months it has managed to broadcast uninterrupted on its new medium wave frequency from 7 a.m. to midnight. It is loved by the Greek Cypriot community, and unloved by the Government, the Independent Broadcasting Authority, and in particular by the commercial station LBC, which broadcasts on a waveband only a twiddle of a knob away.

The station has applied to the Home Office and the IBA for a licence: 'We want to be legal', says George Eracleous, one of the founders, 'I'm sure we could survive commercially.'

Until now, their efforts have met resistance, but their chances improved dramatically last week when it emerged that the Government is planning to encourage the introduction of community radio, probably within two years.

By 1987 existing 'pirate' stations should be able to apply for community licences, as will any group which wants to broadcast to a minority audience. Would-be applicants include Radio Arabia, which is already broadcasting Arab music and Muslim prayers to the 700,000 Muslims in London, and Sea Rock Entertainment, which plans two music stations for the 22,000 people of the Shetlands.

Simon Partridge, secretary of the Community Radio Association, says, 'The trouble is that local radio in Britain is not really local. There are three so-called local stations in London, for instance, covering a 10 million population with enormously different needs and interests. Yet New York has more than 100 radio stations and even Paris is setting up about 50.'

Meanwhile, the existing, legitimate local radio stations will be marshalling strong resistance to the Government's plans. Community radio obviously threatens to hit them where it hurts.

31    What is the most likely reason that people have sent gifts to London Greek Radio?

   A   To demonstrate support for their fight for a licence.

   B   To show appreciation of the Greek programmes.

   C   To encourage them to broadcast more Cypriot programmes.

   D   To persuade them to extend their broadcasting hours.

32 The commercial radio station LBC dislikes London Greek Radio because

    A  it doesn't approve of Greek programmes in London.

    B  the Greek broadcasts interfere with their own programmes.

    C  it fears the public will prefer the Greek programmes.

    D  it disapproves of illegal broadcasting.

33 Why were the London Greek Radio transmitters frequently confiscated?

    A  The station had no licence.

    B  They broadcast on another station's waveband.

    C  Only three radio stations are allowed in London.

    D  The Government disapproves of community radio.

34 Community radio stations are generally for the benefit of

    A  non-English speakers.

    B  island dwellers.

    C  minority groups.

    D  music lovers.

35 What is the writer of this passage attempting to do?

    A  Clearly explain a very complicated situation.

    B  Show how unreasonable the Government's attitude is.

    C  Point out the public's indifference to 'pirate' radio.

    D  Gain sympathy for the community radio stations.

## THIRD PASSAGE

*Extract 1*

**London Chamber of Commerce and Industry Examination Board**

Founded in the 1880s to set targets in the business education field, the Board now examines some 23,000 EFL candidates annually in UK and overseas using: ENGLISH FOR COMMERCE: Written, available 4 times per year at 3 levels – Elementary, Intermediate, Higher – with short oral tests at I and H levels. A new syllabus, under the name of ENGLISH FOR BUSINESS, is being introduced in 1988.

SPOKEN ENGLISH FOR INDUSTRY AND COMMERCE: Purely oral, available at any time on any suitable premises with one month's notice, at 4 levels – Preliminary, Threshold, Intermediate and Advanced.

*Extract 2*
## Royal Society of Arts Examinations Board
The RSA Examinations in the Communicative Use of English as a Foreign Language (CUEFL) assess what students can do with English rather than what they *know* about English. The tasks in the examination are therefore as realistic as possible. They are offered at three levels and the specifications say exactly what is expected at each level. There are separate exams testing skills of writing, reading, listening and oral interaction, so that students can take any skill at any level according to their needs. They are available twice a year in the UK and at recognised centres abroad. There is a separate scheme for students of English as a second language.

*Extract 3*
## University of Cambridge Local Examinations Syndicate
Cambridge EFL examining represents a natural development from over a century of involvement with school examinations overseas. It is essentially a large-scale, internationally conceived operation seeking to combine innovation and relevance to teaching and learning needs with administrative viability. Syllabus design concentrates on a computer-monitored balance between objective and open-ended testing, using each as a check on the other, and a similar balance between communicative and analytical factors in candidate performance.

*Extract 4*
## Associated Examining Board
The AEB's Test in English for Educational Purposes (TEEP) is based, following extensive analysis, on the linguistic needs of students entering HE or FE, where they will study through the medium of English. It tests Listening, Reading, Writing and (optionally) Speaking. The approach is communicative, with many subtests being integrated, for example, a reading passage is linked thematically with a listening exercise, and they both lead to a writing task. The Oral, recorded on tape, tests responses to social and academic situations and ability to participate in discussion, offer opinion, ask questions and to summarize relevantly. TEEP is recognized as acceptable by FE.

36   What do extracts 1 and 2 have in common?

   A   Examinations are offered at three different levels.

   B   All four language skills are tested.

   C   Oral tests are given at three levels.

   D   Examinations are available four times a year.

37   Both extracts 1 and 3 show that the examination boards

   A   concentrate mainly on overseas candidates.

   B   have developed language tests from other examinations.

   C   are more than one hundred years old.

   D   are part of large international organisations.

38   Extracts 2 and 4 share the opinion that

   A   candidates should be tested on their knowledge of English.

   B   their examinations should prepare students for further study.

   C   the communicative approach to testing is most important.

   D   speaking is the least important of the four language skills.

39   The thematic linking of subjects explained in extract 4 is likely to

   A   present a realistic way of testing language.

   B   lead to confusion among the candidates.

   C   cause problems in assessing results.

   D   facilitate linguistic analysis.

40   Compared with extracts 1, 2 and 4, extract 3 is the most

   A   informative.

   B   generalised.

   C   academic.

   D   analytic.

# PAPER 2   COMPOSITION   (2 hours)

*Write* **two only** *of the following composition exercises. Your answers must follow exactly the instructions given. Write in pen, not pencil. You are allowed to make alterations, but see that your work is clear and easy to read.*

1   Suggest some ways of improving life for unemployed people. (About 350 words)

2   'The world is a very dangerous place to live in nowadays.' Discuss. (About 350 words)

3   Write a story entitled 'The Revenge'. (About 350 words)

4   In a recent talk on the radio it was implied that fat people are less loveable than thin ones. You object to several of the points put forward, that fat people:

> look unattractive
> dress badly
> think slowly
> are uninteresting
> lack imagination
> are bad lovers
> have inadequate personalities

Write a letter of protest of about 300 words to the producer about the biased nature of the programme.

5   (See Appendix: Prescribed texts)

# PAPER 3   USE OF ENGLISH   (2 hours)

*Answer **all** the questions.*
*Your answers must be written in ink in this booklet, using the spaces provided.*

## SECTION A

1   *Fill in each of the numbered blanks in the following passage with **one** suitable word.*

On a recent visit to ........................... (1) of America's larger electronic shows, I came ........................... (2) some really oddball telephones.

One ........................... (3) was the can telephone which had a body in the ........................... (4) of a metal drinks can, the exterior was ........................... (5) to look like a can of Coke or 7-Up. A small handset ........................... (6) on the side of the can.

Or, ........................... (7) about the 'Crusader Frog Phone'? Seated on the table it looked a rather attractive modern ........................... (8) of a frog. ........................... (9) pick it up, and it unfolds into a telephone handset ........................... (10) with push-button dialling. ........................... (11) opened the frog's eyes ........................... (12) red and ........................... (13) dialling, twinkle in ........................... (14) to the dialling signal. After ........................... (15) extravagance, I was ........................... (16) relieved to encounter 'Hotlips', a bright scarlet plastic sculpture of a ........................... (17) of lips. ........................... (18) up the top lip and it ........................... (19) a handset; the push-button dialling panel ........................... (20) revealed in the lower lip.

2  *Finish each of the following sentences in such a way that it means exactly the same as the sentence printed before it.*

> EXAMPLE:   He didn't seem to want to leave.
>
> ANSWER:   He seemed *to want to stay.*

a)  'Don't ever do that again', the mother told her son.
The son .....................................................................................................................

b)  It is quite useless telling her anything.
There's .....................................................................................................................

c)  My garage needs painting.
It's time .....................................................................................................................

d)  The security guard refused to allow the man to enter the bank.
'You can't .....................................................................................................................

e)  It's against the law to park your car there.
Your .....................................................................................................................

f)  The director was looking for a woman with advertising experience.
A woman .....................................................................................................................

g)  I haven't smoked for ten years.
I stopped .....................................................................................................................

h)  That Fiat is still up for sale.
Nobody .....................................................................................................................

3  *Fill each of the blanks with a suitable word or phrase.*

> EXAMPLE:   I wouldn't have been able to go even *if I had had the* .................... money.

a)  She suggested going to the concert ................................................................ he
hated modern music.

b)  I wish ........................................................................ , he wears me out.

c)  It's quicker to go by train but ........................................................................ bus.

d)  Do I ........................................................................ to the station to meet her?

e)  Sorry, I'm late. I hope ........................................................................ long.

f)  She doesn't like cleaning windows, she'd rather ........................................................................
.................... by the window cleaner.

4    *For each of the sentences below, write a new sentence* **as similar as possible in meaning to the original sentence,** *but using the word given. This word must* **not be altered** *in any way.*

EXAMPLE:    Do you have to do military service in your country?
**compulsory**

ANSWER:    *Is military service compulsory in your country?*
..............................................................................................................................

a)    By no means are you to leave early.
**account**

..............................................................................................................................

b)    When I was a child I was a hopscotch champion.
**used**

..............................................................................................................................

c)    Her choice of friends displeases me.
**care**

..............................................................................................................................

d)    He was determined to have his own way.
**mind**

..............................................................................................................................

e)    Be careful that you don't lose the money.
**whatever**

..............................................................................................................................

f)    He always turns a deaf ear to my requests.
**never**

..............................................................................................................................

g)    I must say he doesn't waste time on the job.
**gets**

..............................................................................................................................

h)    Everything was very peaceful at the demonstration.
**sign**

..............................................................................................................................

## SECTION B

5   *Read the following passage, and then answer the questions which follow it.*

There is no doubt that the future is, and always has been, one of the most seductive subjects to which the human mind can turn. Anyone who has ever whiled away a dull or sleepless hour in the pastime of planning – whether for next summer's flower garden, a new home, a fortune-spinning business, or a vacation – will know just how
5   engaging the future becomes when reality can be completely ignored or temporarily tamed into compliance with fantasy.

Fortunately, maturity brings a healthy scepticism to temper that kind of euphoria. Experience teaches that tomorrow's gardens, homes, business deals, and vacations turn out to be much like yesterday's. We can make believe it will be otherwise without
10   too much harm; but if we truly believe it, we are behaving more like compulsive gamblers than like shrewd managers of affairs. Then, too, the nature of an unbridled daydream, the fact that it occupies time out of our more sober and useful workday lives, helps to devaluate it in advance.

But what of futurologists – those who make a profession of forecasting the future?
15   Around the world there must by now be several thousand practitioners of this new science, men and women who devote their working lives to devising and refining techniques for predicting the broad future. And for every one of these there are a further 1,000, if not 10,000, whose concern is some particular aspect of that broad future. Their field may be global, such as the future of the energy industries, or it may
20   be literally parochial, such as the traffic pattern round the village green five years from now. The futurologists are people with a full or part-time professional concern with the future; someone pays them to make predictions and suggest courses of action on the basis of their expectations.

The predictions they make are not of the daytime kind (although 'daytime
25   nightmare' might aptly characterise some of their findings), nor are they much concerned with the utterly unguessable long-term future – a century or more ahead, say. As for the very long-term future, we actually know a great deal about it, and there is little point in concerning ourselves with it. Here for instance are some of its certainties:

30   The sun will explode spectacularly as either a nova or supernova, or else it will swell and cool slightly, becoming a red giant. Either type of event will destroy the Earth as we know it.
Earth and Moon will collide.
The present arrangement of continents and oceans will change beyond recognition.
35   Most, if not all, of the existing species will eventually become extinct, supplanted by the new forms which will evolve from the present ones.
Predictions of such far-off and inescapable happenings will make little impression upon us, and in no way can condition our daily lives. Nobody is likely to change his ways because Earth and Moon will one day collide; few would pay more for his hilltop
40   land because it will be spared from flooding when Antarctica melts. But the short-term future, upon which the futurologists focus most of their attention, is quite another thing. If we do not manage to survive the short-term – the next 10 to 25 years – there can be no long-term worries anyhow.

a) Why is it suggested in the first paragraph that thinking about the future is seductive?

..............................................................................................................................

b) Explain the phrase 'whiled away a dull or sleepless hour' (lines 2–3).

..............................................................................................................................

c) What word could replace 'engaging' (line 5)?

..............................................................................................................................

d) What is being 'temporarily tamed into compliance' (lines 5–6)? What is the meaning of this phrase?

..............................................................................................................................

e) What exactly is the 'euphoria' referred to (line 7)?

..............................................................................................................................

f) What does 'it' refer to (line 9)?

..............................................................................................................................

g) What is meant by 'an unbridled daydream' (lines 11–12)?

..............................................................................................................................

h) What is the 'new science' referred to (lines 15–16)?

..............................................................................................................................

i) Explain 'literally parochial' (line 20).

..............................................................................................................................

j) What do you think are the futurologist's findings described as a 'daytime nightmare' (lines 24–5)?

..............................................................................................................................

k) The long-term future does not concern futurologists very much. Why not?

..............................................................................................................................

l) What does 'its certainties' refer to (lines 28–9)?

..............................................................................................................................

m) What is suggested will happen to mankind in the far-off future?

..............................................................................................................................

n)     In a paragraph of 50 – 80 words summarise man's interest in futurology.

     ........................................................................................................................................................

     ........................................................................................................................................................

     ........................................................................................................................................................

     ........................................................................................................................................................

     ........................................................................................................................................................

# PAPER 4 LISTENING COMPREHENSION (Approx. 30 minutes)

*Further instructions will be given on the recording. Your answers must be written in ink in this booklet, using the spaces provided.*

## FIRST PART

*For question 1 write your answers in the spaces provided. For question 2 tick the appropriate boxes i – vi.*

1 The speaker mentions three conditions in a mother, other than posture or movement, which could lead to the development of back pain. What are they?

    (i)   ......................................................................................................................................

   (ii)   ......................................................................................................................................

 (iii)   ......................................................................................................................................

2 Indicate which of the following things the speaker mentions about processed foods which make them *inadequate* for a balanced diet.

    (i)   They contain preservatives. ☐

   (ii)   They lack colour. ☐

 (iii)   They go stale easily. ☐

 (iv)   They have emulsifiers added. ☐

  (v)   They are synthetic. ☐

 (vi)   They have natural vitamins added. ☐

*For questions 3–6 put a tick in one of the boxes A, B, C or D.*

3 The speaker when talking about posture, states that carrying a child on the hip can result in damage to the mother's back. Which of the four drawings shows the back pain area?

A ☐      B ☐      C ☐      D ☐

4    What is it suggested that women should practise doing?

    A    Bending from the waist.

    B    Bending from the knees.

    C    Bending forwards.

    D    Bending sideways.

| |
|---|
| A |
| B |
| C |
| D |

5    Which of the following should be done from a kneeling position?

    A    Bathing the baby.

    B    Picking up the baby.

    C    Making the beds.

    D    Cleaning the sink.

| |
|---|
| A |
| B |
| C |
| D |

6    The biggest problem for women bringing up children alone is

    A    having too much work to do.

    B    not being able to get nutritious food.

    C    having to lift heavy weights.

    D    taking risks with their health.

| |
|---|
| A |
| B |
| C |
| D |

## SECOND PART

*For questions 7–16, tick whether each statement is true or false.*

| | True | False |
|---|---|---|
| 7   Tony has recently gone to live in the country. | | |
| 8   He went to live in the country because he lost his job. | | |
| 9   He studied for a social work diploma for two years. | | |
| 10   He decided to move to the country because he liked the scenery. | | |
| 11   His first problem was finding somewhere to live. | | |
| 12   He didn't buy a smallholding because they were too expensive. | | |
| 13   He first started up his nursery in a small cottage. | | |
| 14   Nobody went to the nursery in the beginning because the fruit and flowers didn't grow very fast. | | |
| 15   The most successful advertising of the nursery was on local radio. | | |
| 16   Tony says the most important quality needed when you start your own business is perseverence. | | |

### THIRD PART

*For questions 17–19, tick* **one** *of the boxes A, B, C or D.*

17  This announcment is being made at a

    A   sports centre.

    B   department store.

    C   health clinic.

    D   gymnasium.

| A |
|---|
| B |
| C |
| D |

18  What is the practical advantage of the Sunshine Sunbed?

    A   It gives you a quick tan.

    B   It has an up-to-date design.

    C   It's battery-operated.

    D   It's easy to move.

| A |
|---|
| B |
| C |
| D |

19  Anyone who wants to test the sunbed for themselves will receive a

    A   free drink.

    B   pair of sunglasses.

    C   free skin test.

    D   bottle of suntan lotion.

| A |
|---|
| B |
| C |
| D |

## PAPER 5 INTERVIEW  (Approx. 15 minutes)

*Look at this photograph carefully and be prepared to describe and discuss it.*

a) Describe the man kneeling down.
    the picture.
    the place.

b) Different art forms.
   The working environment.
   Graffiti.

c) *Study one or more of the following passages and be prepared to answer questions or make comments on the subject matter.*

   (i) 'Although there is good work being done in the conventional arts – painting, sculpture, music, dance, poetry, etc., the newest energies are gathering in the crossovers, the areas of impurity, the blurs which remain after the usual boundaries have been eased. This zone is increasingly referred to as 'intermedia' and within this zone I see the most critical point of oscillation occurring between intermedia and life.'

(ii) 'Photography, the new medium of the last century, helped to drive painting away from representation. Today there is an alternative view of reality, a computer simulation. It is the characteristics of computer image-making that I am incorporating into my language of painting, just as some artists of the past took the vision of the camera as a new viewpoint for their art.'

(iii) The term 'oil painting' refers to more than a technique. It defines an art form. The technique of mixing pigments with oil had existed since the ancient world. But the oil painting as an art form was not born until there was a need to develop and perfect this technique in order to express a particular view of life for which the techniques of tempera or fresco were inadequate.

d) General discussion:

*Single candidate*
Study two of the pictures on the theme of eating and comment on the contrasting treatment of the subject.

*Group*
Compare and contrast one of the pictures with the pictures of other members of the group.

A TEA GARDEN

*and/or*

e)  Debate:

*Study the topic and be prepared to speak for or against the motion. One, or more, of the following themes may help you in the preparation of your speech(es).*

Topic:  **Is Art important in the modern world?**

Themes:  Man does not live by bread alone.
Does technology nourish the spirit?
Seeing comes before speaking.
Art passes on cultural values.
Life is short but Art is long.
Art is for the elite and educated.
Technology and design are taking the place of Art.

f)  (See Appendix: Prescribed texts)

# Appendix: Prescribed Texts

Candidates may choose one of the questions on prescribed books as a basis for one topic in Paper 2 (Composition) and one for the Paper 5 (Interview).
The texts set for 1987 are:

*The Talented Mr Ripley*     Patricia Highsmith
*The Entertainer*     John Osborne
*Selected Tales*     D. H. Lawrence (Ed. Serraillier, Heinemann)

Different texts may be substituted from year to year for one or all of the books prescribed. Candidates should be reminded that only one of these topics can be chosen for Paper 2 (Composition). The other must be selected from topics 1–4.
Following are examples of the kind of topic the candidate may be asked to deal with on prescribed books:

**THE TALENTED MR RIPLEY**

**COMPOSITION (Paper 2)** *(About 350 words)*

*Basing your answer on your reading of the book, answer* **one** *of the following.*

a)   How important was Tom Ripley's talent for impersonation?

b)   What events led up to the murder of Freddie?

c)   What had happened in Tom's childhood to turn him into a murderer?

### INTERVIEW (Paper 5)

a)   *Consider the book cover for* The Talented Mr Ripley *and comment on how it relates to the story.* (see Figure 1, Page 105)

b)   *Study the following passages and be prepared to comment on one or more of them with reference to the characters, plot and storyline of the novel.*

 (i)   Tom remained standing, his hands at his sides, his head high. In a large mirror on the wall he could see himself: the upright, self-respecting young man again. He looked quickly away. He was doing the right thing, behaving the right way. Yet he had a feeling of guilt. When he had said to Mrs Greenleaf just now, *I'll do everything I can.* . . Well, he meant it. He wasn't trying to fool anybody.

 (ii)   Tom had an ecstatic moment when he thought of all the pleasures that lay before him now with Dickie's money, other beds, tables, seas, ships, suitcases, shirts, years of freedom, years of pleasure. Then he turned the light out and put his head down and almost at once fell asleep, happy, content, and utterly confident, as he had never been before in his life.

 (iii)   But if only he could sit tight, nothing at all would happen. It was just this moment he thought, just this little crisis with the boat story and the unsolved Freddie Miles murder, that made things so difficult. But absolutely nothing would happen to him, if he could keep on doing and saying the right things to everybody. Afterwards it would be smooth sailing again.

c) General discussion:

*Choose one or more of the following questions about the book for discussion.*

   (i)   When do signs of Tom Ripley's strangeness first become apparent?

   (ii)  Why should Tom Ripley want to assume another person's persona?

   (iii) Would you describe *The Talented Mr Ripley* as an ordinary thriller? If not, in what way is it different?

## THE ENTERTAINER

### COMPOSITION (Paper 2) *(About 350 words)*

*Basing your answers on your reading of the play, answer* **one** *of the following.*

a) Comment on Archie's despair and say what you think caused it.

b) Why do you think Phoebe and Archie decided to leave England at the end of the play and what events lead up to this decision?

c) In what way has entertainment changed since Billy Rice's day?

### INTERVIEW (Paper 5)

a) *Consider the picture for the cover of the* The Entertainer *and comment on how it relates to the play.* (see Figure 2, Page 106)

b) *Study the following passages and be prepared to comment on one or more of them with reference to the characters, plot and scenes in the play.*

   (i)   No, I haven't seen it. I wouldn't. These nudes. They're killing the business. Anyway, I keep telling him, it's dead already. Has been for years. It was all over, finished, dead when I got out of it. I saw it coming. I saw it coming, and I got out. They don't want real people any more.

   (ii)  And do you know why? Do you know why? Because we're dead beat and down and outs. We're drunks, maniacs, we're crazy, we're bonkers, the whole flaming bunch of us. Why, we have problems that nobody's ever heard of, we're characters out of something that nobody believes in. We're something that people make jokes about, because we're so remote from the rest of ordinary, everyday, human experience. But we're not really funny. We're too boring.

   (iii) Look around you. Can you think of any good reason for staying in this cosy little corner of Europe? Don't kid yourself anyone's going to let you do anything, or try anything here, Jeannie. Because they're not. You haven't got a chance. Who are you – you're nobody. You're nobody, you've no money, and you're young. And when you end up it's pretty certain you'll still be nobody, you'll still have no money – the only difference is you'll be *old*.

c) General discussion:

*Choose one or more of the following questions about the play for discussion.*

(i) Frank acts as a 'straight man' and supports his father's jokes for much of the play. What finally stops him acting like this?

(ii) *The Entertainer* was written in 1956 when Music Hall entertainment was already dead. Why do you think John Osborne gave his play a Music Hall setting?

(iii) Why do you think Archie Rice is so bitter and despairing?

## SELECTED TALES

### COMPOSITION (Paper 2) *(About 350 words)*

*Basing your answer on your reading of the short stories concerned, answer* **one** *of the following.*

a) Explain Paul's strange obsession with his rocking-horse and say what it represents to him.

b) Show how Louisa's 'fixed will to love, to have the man she loves' triumphs in the end.

c) Contrast the life of a mining village as portrayed in 'The Christening' with that described in 'Odour of Chrysanthemums'.

### INTERVIEW (Paper 5)

a) *Consider the book cover for* Selected Tales *by D. H. Lawrence and comment on it.* (see Figure 3, Page 107)

b) *Study the following passages and be prepared to comment on one or more of them with reference to the characters, plot and storyline of the stories.*

(i) For as she looked at the dead man, her mind, cold and detached, said clearly: 'Who am I? What have I been doing? I have been fighting a husband who did not exist. *He* existed all the time. What wrong have I done? What was that I have been living with? There lies the reality, this man.'

(ii) The father sat big and unheeding in his chair, his eyes vacant, his physique wrecked. He let them do as they would, he fell to pieces. And yet some power, involuntary, like a curse, remained in him. The very ruin of him was like a lodestone that held them in its control. The wreck of him still dominated the house, in his dissolution even he compelled their being. They had never lived; his life, his will had always been upon them and contained them. They were only half-individuals.

(iii) Only he still derived his single satisfaction from being alone, absolutely alone, with the space soaking into him. The grey sea alone, and the footing of his sea-washed island. No other contact. Nothing human to bring its horror into contact with him. Only space, damp, twilit, sea-washed space! This was the bread of his soul.

c) General discussion:

*Choose one or more of the following questions about the book for discussion.*

(i) What effect does the accident have on Ephraim in 'Strike-pay'?

(ii) Why did the girls beat John Thomas in 'Tickets, Please'?

(iii) What effect did Miss Stokes have on Joe and Albert's friendship in 'Monkey Nuts'?

Figure 1

Figure 2

# The Entertainer

A Play by John Osborne

With Music by John Addison

Figure 3

UNIVERSITY OF CAMBRIDGE
LOCAL EXAMINATIONS SYNDICATE

# Answer Sheet

PAPER 1   READING COMPREHENSION

NAME ...............................................................................................................................................

**PLEASE READ THESE NOTES CAREFULLY**

1.   Check that this answer sheet has your correct name and index number printed on it

2.   For each question, suggested answers are given on your question paper. CHOOSE ONE LETTER ONLY
for each question, and show your choice clearly ON THIS SHEET.

**MARK
HEAVILY**

EXAMPLE  If you think B is the right letter for Question 1,
fill in the answer sheet like this

    A    B    C    D

**FILL IN
THE
LOZENGES**

3.   **USE ORDINARY PENCIL ONLY** (SOFT - 2B or GRADE 1 PREFERRED)
Any errors must be thoroughly rubbed out using a clean eraser.

| 1  A B C D | 16  A B C D | 31  A B C D |
| 2  A B C D | 17  A B C D | 32  A B C D |
| 3  A B C D | 18  A B C D | 33  A B C D |
| 4  A B C D | 19  A B C D | 34  A B C D |
| 5  A B C D | 20  A B C D | 35  A B C D |
| 6  A B C D | 21  A B C D | 36  A B C D |
| 7  A B C D | 22  A B C D | 37  A B C D |
| 8  A B C D | 23  A B C D | 38  A B C D |
| 9  A B C D | 24  A B C D | 39  A B C D |
| 10  A B C D | 25  A B C D | 40  A B C D |
| 11  A B C D | 26  A B C D | |
| 12  A B C D | 27  A B C D | |
| 13  A B C D | 28  A B C D | |
| 14  A B C D | 29  A B C D | |
| 15  A B C D | 30  A B C D | |

**SHOW YOUR ANSWERS ON THIS SHEET**          **USE PENCIL ONLY**

# ANSWER KEY AND TAPESCRIPT

# Answer Key and Tapescript

## TEST ONE: KEY

### PAPER 1

Section A

| | | | | | | | |
|---|---|---|---|---|---|---|---|
| 1 | C | 10 | D | 18 | B | | |
| 2 | D | 11 | A | 19 | C | | |
| 3 | A | 12 | B | 20 | C | | |
| 4 | B | 13 | A | 21 | D | | |
| 5 | D | 14 | D | 22 | A | | |
| 6 | A | 15 | C | 23 | B | | |
| 7 | B | 16 | B | 24 | C | | |
| 8 | C | 17 | A | 25 | D | | |
| 9 | B | | | | | | |

Section B

*First Passage*

26  C
27  B
28  B
29  D
30  B

*Second Passage*

31  C
32  C
33  B
34  B
35  C

*Third Passage*

36  B
37  A
38  D
39  C
40  B

### PAPER 3

Section A

1
  1  their
  2  one
  3  think/stare/act
  4  us/people/humans
  5  else
  6  Do
  7  that
  8  killing/chasing/slaughter
  9  where/when/if/wherever/whenever
  10  own
  11  this/that
  12  watch/observe
  13  games
  14  balls
  15  off
  16  clawing/leaping/jumping
  17  hand
  18  such/their/many
  19  practise/perfect/rehearse
  20  it/themselves/playing

2 a) He absolutely objects to /loathes travelling by train.
   b) Is it possible to hire a car from the airport?
   c) Would you mind telling me your name again/repeat your name, (please)?
   d) Peter warned his girlfriend not to go too far out because the sea was very rough.
   e) The supermarket doesn't sell stamps.
   f) You'll miss the bus if you don't/unless you hurry up.
   g) They always made me feel uncomfortable when I was with them.
   h) Andrew has told me a lot about you.

3 a) he will have been there for
   b) I wouldn't have got into/be in/have been in
   c) haven't got/don't have one
   d) I'm taking/going to take my
   e) didn't make/hasn't made any
   f) any notice of what

4 a) There are no/aren't any seats/places left in this bus.
   b) He had/was given/got a two-year jail sentence.
   c) It's too much trouble to write those letters today.
   d) Have you ever had/Did you have a teaching job before?
   e) It's important that you (should) arrive on time in the morning.
   f) He is trying to lose weight.
   g) I met them (just) by chance.
   h) With your blond hair, you could pass for a Scandinavian.


## Section B

5 *Candidates' answers to these questions may vary considerably in structure, expression and interpretation of the passage. Candidates should, however, be able to demonstrate comprehension of the gist of the passage and the writer's intentions and an understanding of particular words or phrases. The following are suggested answers:*

   a) The first novel with the character Bond was not written by the original author, Ian Fleming.
   b) The characters which (because of their popularity) appear in books by new authors written after the death of the original author.
   c) Because Bond sometimes literally does float in the films where special effects are used.
   d) There was a skillful mixture of realism and extravagance.
   e) Because it was easier to accept the extravagance if there was also an element of realism and vice versa.
   f) The description of the character as unusual and unattractive.
   g) That the absurdity is very exaggerated.
   h) The Bond of the novels was a mixture of realism and extravagance whilst the element of realism was missing in the films.
   i) The readers thought that the films were childish and many of the viewers hadn't ever heard of the books. Those viewers who had, thought of them as material to be ridiculed.
   j) ' . . . their almost mesmeric readability . . . '
   k) He thinks the style is bad but nevertheless very readable.
   l) Because all of Bond's movements and plans are known by the opposition well in advance.
   m) *Main points*: in twenty years since Fleming's creation of Bond, character changed immensely; used to be a mixture of realism and extravagance; Sir Hugo Drax as an example of this; original Bond novels are extremely readable despite their similar plots; Bond himself not impressive in organisational skills since his plans are discovered well in advance.

## PAPER 4

| First Part | | Second Part | | Third Part | | Fourth Part | |
|---|---|---|---|---|---|---|---|
| 1 | *The Fisher Line* | 10 | C | 14 | Records | 23 | C |
| 2 | Anthony Daniels | 11 | D | 15 | Boots and shoes | 24 | D |
| 3 | Thursday afternoon/Friday morning | 12 | C | 16 | Books | 25 | B |
| 4 | £9.95 | 13 | C | 17 | Department store | | |
| 5 | Cash | | | 18 | Prints and pictures | | |
| 6 | A | | | 19 | Chain store | | |
| 7 | D | | | 20 | Men's clothes | | |
| 8 | A | | | 21 | Shoes | | |
| 9 | D | | | 22 | Electrical, hi-fi | | |

# TEST ONE: TAPESCRIPT

## FIRST PART

*In the first part of the test you are going to hear a telephone conversation between a bookshop assistant and a customer. Turn to Pages 13–14 of your test book. For questions 1–5 you should fill in the correct answer. For questions 6–9 tick one of the boxes A, B, C or D. You will hear the piece twice.*

*(Telephone ringing)*

| | |
|---|---|
| SHOP ASSISTANT | Clifton's Bookshop. |
| MACDONALD | Good morning, I'd like to order a book. |
| SHOP ASSISTANT | What's the title? |
| MACDONALD | Well, I'm not sure – I don't remember exactly – *The Fisherman* – I think. |
| SHOP ASSISTANT | *The Fisherman*? Who's it by? |
| MACDONALD | Anthony Daniels, I believe. |
| SHOP ASSISTANT | Anthony Daniels. Oh, you mean *The Fisher Line*. |
| MACDONALD | Oh, of course – *The Fisher Line*. I always get titles mixed up. |
| SHOP ASSISTANT | Now, let's see, it's published by Nelson at £9.95 in hardback. |
| MACDONALD | Oh, don't you have it in paperback? I only want it for my English Lit. exam. |
| SHOP ASSISTANT | No, it isn't published in paperback yet, and I'm afraid we haven't got a copy of the hardback edition but I can order it for you if you like. |
| MACDONALD | Oh yes, you'd better. Er, when could you get it by? |
| SHOP ASSISTANT | Well, it's Tuesday today. I could probably get it for you by Thursday afternoon, or Friday morning at the latest. |
| MACDONALD | Mmm, the exam's on Monday – that doesn't leave me very much time to read it. What a bore. |
| SHOP ASSISTANT | Would you like me to order it for you? |
| MACDONALD | Yes please, I've got to have it, and I need it as soon as possible. |
| SHOP ASSISTANT | If you'd just give me your name . . .<br>. . . and how would you like to pay? Cheque or credit card? |
| MACDONALD | Well, actually, I haven't got a credit card, and I don't really want to pay by cheque. It's a bit near the end of term and my bank manager gets rather irate if I overdraw. I'll pay cash. £9.95, you said? What a shocking price! |
| SHOP ASSISTANT | It's only just come out and new books are expensive. Now, I'll give you a ring as soon as the book comes in. Will there be anybody there to take a message if you're out? |
| MACDONALD | Well, there's usually someone at the hostel, or there's a board in the hall where we stick messages for each other – there isn't a receptionist or anything. |

| SHOP ASSISTANT | Well, if you don't get the message, perhaps you could ring me and arrange to come in and pick it up on Thursday afternoon or Friday morning. |
| MACDONALD | I can't manage Thursday, I've got to see my tutor, so it'll have to be Friday morning. You open at nine, don't you? |
| SHOP ASSISTANT | No, ten o'clock. |
| MACDONALD | Oh well, ten then. Thanks very much. |
| SHOP ASSISTANT | Thank you, goodbye. |

## SECOND PART

*For the second part of the test you will hear two people talking about an accident. Look at Page 14 of your test book. You should tick one of the boxes A, B, C or D. You will hear the piece twice.*

| INTERVIEWER | When did you first notice that the boy was in difficulties, Harry? |
| HARRY | Well, I was fishing from the bridge, as I generally do on Saturdays, when I saw this kid come out from under the bridge in a rowing boat. He seemed to be weaving all over the place and it looked as if the oars were too heavy for him. I was just going to call out to him to keep away from my line when he lost one of his oars. He leaned over to get it and the boat capsized. It was as simple as that. |
| INTERVIEWER | What did you do then? |
| HARRY | Well, I saw him struggling in the water and then he went under. I thought, 'My God, he can't swim!' |
| INTERVIEWER | So you jumped off the bridge to save him? |
| HARRY | There wasn't much else I could do, was there? |
| INTERVIEWER | But that's a hell of a jump – four metres, I should say. Talk about dicing with death! |
| HARRY | I don't know about that. I didn't stop to think how far it was to the water. I know I hit the river with an almighty smack and for a moment I thought I'd had it, but then I saw the lad come up, so I grabbed hold of him and sort of pushed and pulled him to the bank. |
| INTERVIEWER | You've never had any training in life-saving then? |
| HARRY | Me? No, I'm not much of a swimmer at the best of times. Still, I got him out. That was the main thing. |
| INTERVIEWER | What sort of condition was the boy in when you got him to the bank? |
| HARRY | Well, he'd swallowed some water and he was scared stiff, but otherwise he was OK. |
| INTERVIEWER | So, what happened then? |
| HARRY | I carried him to my car and took him to hospital; we dripped water all over Casualty for a bit, but there was nothing much wrong with him, so, after a while, they let him go home. |
| INTERVIEWER | Well, I know Johnny's parents are deeply grateful to you for saving their boy's life. You must feel very proud of yourself. |
| HARRY | Not really. Anyone would have done the same. You could hardly let the kid drown, could you? |

## THIRD PART

*Listen to the following telephone conversation between a tourist guide and a visitor to London. Look at the plan on Page 15. Listen carefully and write in the boxes what goods the shops specialise in or what types of shops they are. You will hear the conversation twice.*

*(Telephone ringing)*

| GUIDE | London Tourist Information Service. Can I help you? |
| VISITOR | Yes, I'm a visitor to London and I should like some information about the shops. Er . . . where I can buy certain goods. |

GUIDE      Certainly, madam. What particular articles have you in mind?

VISITOR    Well, I should like to buy something for my boyfriend . . . clothes, I think. Can you recommend a good men's clothes shop?

GUIDE      As you can imagine there are a great many clothes shops in London, so perhaps I can suggest you shop in one street, say Oxford Street, or you'll get very tired walking around.

VISITOR    Oh, thank you, that's a good idea. So what men's clothes shops should I try in Oxford Street.

GUIDE      Well, there are a number of department stores, John Lewis, D. H. Evans, Selfridges, all with good men's departments, as well as a wide range of other goods. Then there are the more specialist shops, catering for the younger man, such as The Squire Shop which has a good selection of fashionable men's clothes. And finally, there are one or two chain stores, the most famous probably being Marks and Spencers, and then there's British Home Stores, Littlewoods, and C and A which specialise in modern fashion but at very reasonable prices.

VISITOR    Thanks, that's a wonderful choice. I might have a look at them all. Now, next I need to buy a record or cassette for my younger brother. Where can I get that?

GUIDE      There's HMV near Bond St. Station and the biggest one, Virgin Megastore near Tottenham Court Road. Is that all?

VISITOR    No, there are one or two more things. First, a small radio, not too expensive.

GUIDE      Right, well all the department stores have electrical departments, or there is Lasky's which sell all electrical, hi-fi, TV, video and radio goods.

VISITOR    Oh good. Next I'd like a good bookshop.

GUIDE      Selfridges have a good book department or Claude Gill near Tottenham Court Road is a large shop with a varied range of books. There are other bookshops of course, but not in Oxford Street.

VISITOR    Umm, well I think I'll stay in the one street. Now I'd like some shoes for myself, a print or reproduction picture for my mother and, oh yes, perhaps some perfume as well.

GUIDE      Oxford Street is famous for its shoeshops and there are several all along the street. It's best just to wander along and look so I'll just mention two. Firstly Anello and Davide who specialise in ballet shoes and expensive, but beautifully made shoes, and Lilley and Skinner's which have also got quite an expensive range of shoes. For perfume you can go to the department stores again or to one of the big chemists such as Boots or Underwoods and finally for a print or picture, there is a wide selection at Athena Reproductions.

VISITOR    Thank you very much indeed, you have been extremely helpful.

GUIDE      You're welcome. We are here to make your stay in London as pleasant as possible, madam, so I hope you enjoy your shopping trip and will return again. Don't hesitate to call us if you need any further information.

VISITOR    Thank you, I will. Goodbye.

# FOURTH PART

*For the fourth part you will hear a politician speaking. Look at questions 23–25 on Page 16. For each question put a tick in one of the boxes A, B, C or D. You will hear the piece twice.*

Calling all voters! This is Dave Jones, your Freedom for Youth candidate. We are the party of action, not words! The party who guarantees to rid Society of outdated ideas! The party that makes room for fresh policies; policies that work! Now is the time for change, for new ideas, for rebirth!

I'll be at the Town Hall tomorrow evening, 7 o'clock, to talk to *you*, about your hopes for the future, to show how we can help *you*, the voter!

Cast your vote for me, Dave Jones, on Election Day – cast your vote for Freedom of Youth – the party that doesn't back down on its manifesto.

## TEST TWO: KEY

### PAPER 1

#### Section A

| | | | | | | |
|---|---|---|---|---|---|
| 1 | B | 10 | B | 18 | C |
| 2 | D | 11 | B | 19 | B |
| 3 | A | 12 | A | 20 | A |
| 4 | B | 13 | C | 21 | C |
| 5 | C | 14 | D | 22 | D |
| 6 | D | 15 | D | 23 | B |
| 7 | B | 16 | A | 24 | A |
| 8 | B | 17 | D | 25 | B |
| 9 | D | | | | |

#### Section B

| *First Passage* | | *Second Passage* | | *Third Passage* | |
|---|---|---|---|---|---|
| 26 | D | 31 | A | 36 | D |
| 27 | C | 32 | C | 37 | C |
| 28 | A | 33 | B | 38 | B |
| 29 | A | 34 | C | 39 | D |
| 30 | A | 35 | A | 40 | C |

### PAPER 3

#### Section A

| 1 | 1 | winner | 11 | pleased/hoping/delighted/surprised |
|---|---|---|---|---|
| | 2 | under | 12 | Director |
| | 3 | aged | 13 | just |
| | 4 | flying/circling/soaring | 14 | picture/painting |
| | 5 | portrayed/reflected/captured/gave | 15 | great/much |
| | 6 | associated | 16 | winning/receiving |
| | 7 | colour/darkness/blackness/tone | 17 | on |
| | 8 | gathering | 18 | prize |
| | 9 | with | 19 | shown/displayed/hung |
| | 10 | light/rays/glow | 20 | Gallery/Museum/Show |

2  a)  I doubt (if/whether) he'll get the job.
   b)  You shouldn't always believe what he says/him.
   c)  He earns less than £6,000 a year.
   d)  I couldn't decide/think/work out what to do.
   e)  I'm not very interested in antiques.
   f)  The meeting ended in uproar.
   g)  Numerous attempts have been made to salvage the treasure.
   h)  What was the reason he said/his reason for saying that?/What made him say that?

**3** a) I'm afraid you're sitting in/you've taken
   b) it'll be too heavy
   c) having/going to have
   d) ought to see/had better see/should see
   e) shouldn't have
   f) I pour/make/get
   g) been telling/told

**4** a) You'll never have an/another opportunity/a chance to hear this great singer (again).
   b) It was up to me to decide/make the decision/No one else could make my mind up.
   c) I don't think we'll ever find a way of solving this problem.
   d) He was in no condition to drive.
   e) Didn't she apologise for keeping/having kept you waiting?
   f) The first thing I did when I got to Heathrow was (to) telephone my office.
   g) The violence at the match was beyond control.
   h) Did he say anything about his new boss in his letter?

## Section B

**5** *Candidates' answers to these questions may vary considerably in structure, expression and interpretation of the passage. Candidates should, however, be able to demonstrate comprehension of the gist of the passage and the writer's intentions and an understanding of particular words or phrases. The following are suggested answers:*

   a) To convey a sense of excess by using a strong image.
   b) A train passenger is free to move around, read, drink, watch the scenery and so on in quiet and comfort unlike those who travel by air or by car.
   c) This metaphor shows that the writer feels as if he's restricted when he has to wear a seatbelt in a car.
   d) In a plane you are strapped in and you are unable to escape from your neighbour. The music, films, and alcohol are a bit too much and, combined with the time change, can leave you exhausted.
   e) The entertainment, drink and time change.
   f) Because as you watch it go past, it changes. The changing view framed in the window is similar to a film on a screen.
   g) The contrast of life inside and outside the train.
   h) In a car or plane you don't have access to your luggage as easily as in a train.
   i) The opportunity for discussion about business and personal life.
   j) Because they don't like talking on long distance journeys.
   k) They lack comfort and style and are often crowded with drinkers so many people prefer to purchase their refreshments and return to their seats.
   l) Completely without.
   m) Because the people know they won't meet again so they are less inhibited.
   n) *Main points*: comparative bliss of trains compared with claustrophobic cars; air travel not much better; freedom of train travel; ability to move around and enjoy the scenery without being subjected to in-flight entertainment; opportunity to do as you wish on a train.

| First Part | Second Part | Third Part | | | Fourth Part | |
|---|---|---|---|---|---|---|
| 1  C | 6  True | 16 | (i) | Pension book | 19 | C |
| 2  B | 7  True | | (ii) | Passport or NHS medical | 20 | B |
| 3  D | 8  False | | | card and post-marked | 21 | B |
| 4  A | 9  False | | | letter | 22 | D |
| 5  D | 10  False | | (iii) | Birth certificate and post- | | |
| | 11  False | | | marked letter | | |
| | 12  False | 17 | (i) | Half-price fares on cheap | | |
| | 13  False | | | day and standard day | | |
| | 14  True | | | returns. | | |
| | 15  True | | (ii) | One third off saver tickets | | |
| | | | | and standard single and | | |
| | | | | return tickets. | | |
| | | 18 | (i) | You can take up to four | | |
| | | | | children for only £1 each. | | |
| | | | (ii) | There are certain | | |
| | | | | reductions on Golden Rail | | |
| | | | | holidays. | | |
| | | | (iii) | Reductions on Motorail if | | |
| | | | | you want to take your car. | | |

# TEST TWO: TAPESCRIPT

## FIRST PART

*Listen to the following conversation at an airport car park reception. Look at questions 1–5 in your test book on Pages 32–3 and tick one of the boxes A, B, C or D. You will hear the conversation twice.*

| | |
|---|---|
| CLERK | Good morning, sir. Can I help you? |
| CUSTOMER | I want to make enquiries about leaving my car with you. You see, I'm going abroad, I don't want to take the car but I'll need it when I get back. |
| CLERK | I see, sir. Well, we can offer you full parking facilities for as long as you wish. |
| CUSTOMER | Good. I'm going to Athens for about a couple of weeks. |
| CLERK | Right, so how long do you want to leave the car with us? |
| CUSTOMER | Well, I'm flying to Athens on the 5th and coming back on the 19th – that's fourteen days, isn't it? |
| CLERK | That works out at fifteen days parking, sir. Let me show you our scale of charges. We have a minimum fee of £6.50 but for fifteen days it would only cost you £24.75. |
| CUSTOMER | It says £23.10 here. |
| CLERK | No, sir, that's for fourteen days. If you're going to be away for fourteen nights, you wouldn't be picking up the car for fifteen days. |
| CUSTOMER | Hmm – fifteen it is then. |
| CLERK | Now, if you'll just come this way, sir, we'll complete the booking form. Could I have your name? |
| CUSTOMER | Brown. Donald Brown . . . |
| CLERK | . . . and the make of car, sir? |
| CUSTOMER | Just a Mini Metro. |
| CLERK | Mini Metro. And the colour? We get rather a lot of Mini Metros. |
| CUSTOMER | It's a sort of greenish-grey. I suppose you'd call it green really. |
| CLERK | Green. What's the registration number? |
| CUSTOMER | Oh, KTY 630Y. |

| CLERK | And your car key number? |
|---|---|
| CUSTOMER | I say, is this all really necessary? |
| CLERK | Afraid so, sir. Security, you see. |
| CUSTOMER | Oh, all right. It's FL 243. |
| CLERK | FL 243. |
| CUSTOMER | Look here, this isn't going to take much longer, is it? |
| CLERK | Only another minute or so, sir. Your departure date is May 5th, I think you said. |
| CUSTOMER | Yes, yes, the 5th, that's a Friday. |
| CLERK | Friday, 5th May. Now what time is your flight, sir? |
| CUSTOMER | Ten to twelve, I think. But I'll have to check in about half an hour beforehand. |
| CLERK | Well, we like customers to check their cars in here at least twenty minutes before check-in time. We have a minibus to take you to the airport. It's only about ten minutes drive. |
| CUSTOMER | So, I ought to be here about ten past eleven. |
| CLERK | Well, it's safer before that. We do get very busy. And you're returning on the 19th? |
| CUSTOMER | Yes, that's right. |
| CLERK | And how would you like to pay, sir? |
| CUSTOMER | Oh, by cheque. Who do I make it out to? |
| CLERK | Gatwick Parking Limited. |
| CUSTOMER | And it's £24.75? |
| CLERK | That's right, sir. I'll just give you a receipt. |
| CUSTOMER | Don't bother, I can't wait. There's a traffic warden coming down the street and I'm parked on a double yellow line. |

## SECOND PART

*For the second part of the test you will hear a tourist guide telling visitors about Salisbury Cathedral. Read questions 6–15 on Page 33 in your test book and tick whether the statements are true or false. You will hear the piece twice.*

Good morning, ladies and gentlemen. At the moment you are standing in the close of Salisbury Cathedral which is a perfect example of early English architecture. It is unique among the English Medieval cathedrals as it was planned as a single unit and not over several centuries. Work started on the Cathedral in 1220 and it was finished and the Cathedral consecrated in 1258, so that makes it over 700 years old. If you look up you will see the magnificent spire which is 404 feet high, the tallest in England. It leans about 29 inches and on the floor inside the Cathedral you can see the 'true' position and the present position marked below the spire. But don't worry, the angle is nothing compared to that achieved by the Leaning Tower of Pisa in Italy. However, such was the combined weight of the tower and the spire, that the four main columns began to bend, so in the 14th and 15th centuries additional arches had to be put in to take the strain; otherwise the building would have collapsed altogether.

Now, just before we enter the Cathedral, if you look over there, just inside the gateway you will see the Matron's College. A very fine building, thought to have been designed by Sir Christopher Wren as a home for widows of the clergy.

Come along into the Cathedral now. Anyone who would like a guide can purchase a copy at the bookstall – then you will be able to follow our route in the booklet as I take you around. You'll find a plan of the Cathedral at the front. Ahead of you is the nave, one of the Cathedral's most striking architectural features; it gives an uninterrupted view throughout the entire 449 foot length of the Cathedral. Around the walls there are several interesting chapels, tombs and memorials, including that of William Longespee, one of the witnesses to the signing of Magna Carta and the first Earl of Salisbury. Over here, you can see the remains of Saint Osmund's shrine. Unfortunately, we can no longer see the original which stood in the Lady Chapel and was covered in gold and jewels. Saint Osmund was thought to have had the power of healing, so pilgrims used to come here and push their diseased limbs through the holes in the base of the shrine and pray to be cured. But we have no knowledge whether any successful cures were achieved. Now, to see the Magna Carta itself, we must go to the

Cathedral library, so come this way . . . This library was founded in Old Sarum in 1089 and moved here when the Cathedral was built. It is noted for its priceless collection of old books and manuscripts and includes one of the three existing legible originals of the Magna Carta; this Salisbury document, it is believed, is the best preserved of the three. As you probably know, the Magna Carta was signed in 1215 by King John and it gave the British their first form of democracy. It was the first time that the rights of the common people to own land and have a say in how the country was run were ever set out and agreed. Finally, before we leave the Cathedral, of great interest is this remarkable ancient clock mechanism dating from about 1386. It is still working, and is said to be the oldest working clock in the country and possibly the world.

Well, ladies and gentlemen, I hope you enjoyed your visit to Salisbury Cathedral, and when you leave *do* notice some of the fine old houses that surround the Cathedral . . .

## THIRD PART

*You will hear a British Rail official speaking with a man about a special railcard. Answer questions 16–18 on Page 34 in your test book. You will hear the conversation twice.*

OFFICIAL  British Rail.

MAN  Good morning, can you tell me how I can get a Senior Citizen Railcard.

OFFICIAL  Yes, well you must be 60 or over and you need to fill in an application form and take it to your nearest mainline railway station or local post office.

MAN  I see. Now, how much does it cost?

OFFICIAL  That depends on the kind of journeys you want to make. For example, if you intend to make long journeys and stay away from home – it's £12, but for short day trips you can get a card for £7.

MAN  Right. Do I need proof of my age?

OFFICIAL  Yes, you must produce your pension book showing you're eligible for a state retirement pension, or a passport or NHS medical card confirming your age plus a postmarked letter addressed to you, or your birth certificate plus a postmarked letter.

MAN  Yes, I've got that. Now, I'm thinking of living abroad now I'm retired, but I shall be coming back to England regularly to visit my children, can I still get a railcard?

OFFICIAL  Certainly, if you have British nationality and live outside the UK you are still eligible as long as you are able to produce the documents as required for UK residents.

MAN  How long does the railcard last?

OFFICIAL  They're valid for one year from the date of issue, and they're easily renewable annually.

MAN  Fine. Now I can travel very cheaply with this card, can't I?

OFFICIAL  Yes, with the £12 card you get half-price fares on both cheap day and standard day returns and a third off saver tickets and standard single and return tickets.

MAN  What about the £7 card?

OFFICIAL  You get the same reductions on cheap and standard day returns but you don't get the third-off benefits.

MAN  I see. Can I also take my wife at a cheap rate on this card?

OFFICIAL  No, I'm afraid not, but you can take up to four children for only £1 each. And there are certain reductions on Golden Rail holidays and the Motorail if you want to take your car with you.

MAN  Well, I think that's everything – Oh wait a moment, where do I get the application form?

OFFICIAL  From your local post office or railway station, but if you have any difficulty just write to us.

MAN  Thanks very much for your help. Goodbye.

## FOURTH PART

*For the fourth part of the test you will hear part of a radio programme. Look at Pages 34–5 in your test book and tick the correct box A, B, C or D. You will hear the piece twice.*

*(Music)*

Hello, you night owls, this is Steve Holly bringing you *After Midnight*, the programme for all you people toiling away while the other lucky ones are snug in bed. First, let me tell you about Night Bus, the competition that may win you the holiday of a lifetime – a trip to a Caribbean island of your choice, no less, and there's lots of consolation prizes. What do you have to do? Well, every night for the next week we're going to give you one clue about a place in or near London, and we want you to identify where that place is. Don't send in your answers until you've heard *all* the clues. And don't phone me, but write your answers on a postcard in the correct order and send them to me at Radio Metro, Victoria Buildings, London SW1. Got that? Radio Metro, Victoria Buildings, London SW1. The first set of correct answers received is the lucky winner. Got your pencil and paper ready? Right – here goes for clue number one:

It's near London.
It's very busy.
It's noisy.
It's a gateway to the world.

Got it? I told you it was easy – and now, how about some night music to keep you all awake . . .

## TEST THREE: KEY

### PAPER 1

#### Section A

| | | | | | |
|---|---|---|---|---|---|
| 1 | B | 10 | C | 18 | D |
| 2 | C | 11 | B | 19 | A |
| 3 | C | 12 | B | 20 | C |
| 4 | A | 13 | B | 21 | C |
| 5 | D | 14 | C | 22 | A |
| 6 | B | 15 | B | 23 | D |
| 7 | D | 16 | B | 24 | B |
| 8 | A | 17 | A | 25 | B |
| 9 | C | | | | |

#### Section B

| *First Passage* | | *Second Passage* | | *Third Passage* | |
|---|---|---|---|---|---|
| 26 | B | 32 | B | 36 | C |
| 27 | D | 33 | D | 37 | D |
| 28 | B | 34 | D | 38 | A |
| 29 | A | 35 | B | 39 | C |
| 30 | D | | | 40 | B |
| 31 | C | | | | |

**PAPER 3**

Section A

1  1  in
   2  deal/extent
   3  only
   4  based/dependent
   5  balance
   6  comes/goes
   7  earning/making/acquiring
   8  loss
   9  ideas/attitudes/aims
   10  own
   11  however
   12  reward(s)/benefits/gain
   13  would/might
   14  blossomed/bloomed
   15  produced/gave/bore
   16  measure(s)/kind
   17  nobody/no one
   18  watching/viewing
   19  almost/nearly/indeed/or/literally
   20  thing

2  a)  There's no point (in) asking John about it.
   b)  The programme will be/is repeated tomorrow evening.
   c)  She takes her work very seriously./She takes great care in her work.
   d)  No one was injured/hurt in the accident.
   e)  I can't go to New York unless I have/without a visa.
   f)  I don't know much about Renaissance art.
   g)  None of the shops are open so I couldn't get any meat.
   h)  Those children never obey/do as they are told.

3  a)  did/does it
   b)  made up your
   c)  nothing for
   d)  not on the
   e)  heard someone
   f)  let me have/take
   g)  the further you
   h)  I always

4  a)  It's unlikely they'll/They're unlikely to be/get here before 10 o'clock.
   b)  My passport is valid until the end of August.
   c)  He's never on time for work.
   d)  The membership of the youth club is restricted to the under 18s.
   e)  All that political jargon is beyond me.
   f)  Did your grandfather leave that old clock to you?
   g)  All our trainees have a compulsory medical test./It is compulsory for all our trainees to have a medical test.
   h)  You're bound to have/come across/experience problems when you start/are starting a new business.

## Section B

5 *Candidates' answers to these questions may vary considerably in structure, expression and interpretation of the passage. Candidates should, however, be able to demonstrate comprehension of the gist of the passage and the writer's intentions and an understanding of particular words or phrases. The following are suggested answers:*

a) Because they hover in mid-air over the embankments.

b) Because they are between the busy traffic and the farmland which has been treated with chemicals.

c) A nature reserve is an area where wildlife is protected. The verges are compared with nature reserves because they support so much wildlife.

d) The soil flourishes because it is free from chemical pesticides.

e) It refers to insects.

f) The nitrogen from the exhaust fumes combines with the soil which supports the plants. The insects which feed on the plants are a source of food for many smaller forms of wildlife such as frogs, toads and small birds. These, in turn, are food for such creatures as kestrels, foxes and badgers.

h) They are evidence of the presence of increasing numbers of wildlife because they prey on small animals.

i) 'debris' is the litter which is thrown away. It is bad because it is not biodegradeable but it is good because it provides homes for small wildlife.

j) The 'hard shoulder' is the lane at the side of the motorway for vehicles when they break down. Crows and hedgehogs are found there because they are looking for food.

k) 'foraging for the corpses' in this context means looking for the insects killed by passing cars which will provide food for crows and hedgehogs.

l) Because the fields had been dug up.

m) *Main points*: Wildlife free from interference from chemicals or disturbance by farm animals; soil is rich in nutrients at the beginning of the food chain so able to support vegetation; wildlife not short of food as a consequence of this and also able to feed on dead insects which bounce off cars; litter from passing cars taken over as homes.

## PAPER 4

| First Part | Second Part | Third Part | Fourth Part |
|---|---|---|---|
| 1 a) 6 | 6 B | 9 Disney World | 20 C |
| b) 1 | 7 C | 10 Sea World | 21 B |
| c) 8 | 8 C | 11 Free | 22 (i) Act 1, Scene 1 |
| d) 4 | | 12 Kennedy Space Center | (ii) Act 2, Scene 3 |
| e) 3 | | 13 Circus World | (iii) Act 2, Scene 4 |
| f) 7 | | 14 Travel home | (iv) Act 2, Scene 2 |
| g) 2 | | 15 C | (v) Act 2, Scene 1 |
| h) 5 | | 16 B | (vi) Act 1, Scene 2 |
| 2 C | | 17 C | |
| 3 C | | 18 A | |
| 4 C | | 19 D | |
| 5 B | | | |

## TEST THREE: TAPESCRIPT

### FIRST PART

*In the first part of the test you are going to hear a conversation between two friends about testing reflexes. For question 1, on Page 53 in your test book put the instructions in the right order. For questions 2–5 tick one of the boxes A, B, C or D. You will hear the conversation twice.*

GEORGE    You know, Brian, test pilots must have incredibly sharp reflexes. I mean, if something goes wrong in the plane they have to react in seconds.

BRIAN    Hmm . . . I know. Actually I've been studying reflexes lately.

GEORGE    Really?

BRIAN    Yes, I've come across this scientific game which tests them.

GEORGE    Scientific game? How does it work?

BRIAN    I'll show you. Have you got a 30 cm ruler and a long sheet of paper?

GEORGE    Yes, I expect so. Look in the top drawer of the desk.

BRIAN    Right, here they are. Oh yes, and some tape. Mind if I use this?

GEORGE    No, go ahead.

BRIAN    Now, what else? Scissors?

GEORGE    There's a pair on the table.

BRIAN    OK – now I want a pen. Hang on, I've got one in my pocket. Now, watch this: I wrap the paper tightly round the ruler and tape the ends down neatly.

GEORGE    I see.

BRIAN    Then, I draw two lines across the width of the paper round the ruler to divide it into three equal parts, then another line about 1 cm from the end – like this.

GEORGE    Hold on, that's four lines in all, isn't it?

BRIAN    Yes, that's right. Now, here's the ruler. Hold it steady for me. I'm going to label the divisions–slow – average – quick – and this small one at the end – test pilot.

GEORGE    OK, so what now?

BRIAN    Give me the ruler back. Hold out your hand – no, not like that. Hold it so the ruler can drop between your index finger and your thumb.

GEORGE    Like this?

BRIAN    That's right. Now I'm going to drop the ruler but I'm not going to tell you when.

GEORGE    What do I do?

BRIAN    Catch it, of course.

GEORGE    What does that prove?

BRIAN    It depends where you catch it. You know if you catch it in the middle that your reflexes are average but if you catch it right at the end then you are good material for a test pilot.

BRIAN    Well, that proves your reflexes are pretty slow!

GEORGE    It was your fault. You didn't warn me that we were going to start yet.

### SECOND PART

*For the second part you will hear a news item. Turn to Page 54 and tick one of the boxes A, B, C or D for questions 6–8. You will hear the item twice.*

The miners' strike shows no sign of being resolved. Leslie Black, their Union Leader, announced their decision not to go to arbitration and their employers, the Coal Board, remain adamant that they will not increase their pay offer above 3%. There were violent clashes between pickets and police at the Bankside Colliery this morning. Five pickets who blocked the road to the colliery with their cars are now in custody. A number of others who attempted to dismantle the winding gear at the pithead were only prevented by the prompt action of the police. We understand that three policemen have been taken to hospital with injuries. A spokesman from the Department of Trade and Industry said that power stations were already running short of coal and that if the strike continued for another two weeks, they could not guarantee that serious power cuts would not be imposed nationwide.

## THIRD PART

*Listen to this conversation and look at Pages 55–6. For questions 9–14 fill in the information about the planned visits. For questions 15–19 put a tick in one of the boxes A, B, C or D. You will hear the conversation twice.*

ANN    I'm longing to hear about this tour you're going on, Lyn. You must be terribly excited.

LYN    Oh, I *am*. I've never been to America before so I'm really looking forward to it. I thought of going fly–drive.

ANN    Fly–drive?

LYN    Yes, you know, you can arrange for a car to be waiting for you at the airport when you arrive – you book everything this end in with the plane ticket.

ANN    Sounds simple enough. Are you going to then?

LYN    Well, I was a bit worried about driving on the other side of the road and having to plan my own route, so I decided it would be better to go on a more organised holiday.

ANN    How do you mean 'organised'?

LYN    Well, everything is arranged by a tour operator, you know, you're taken around and shown where to go and what to do. I'd probably miss half the sights otherwise.

ANN    Um . . . where are you going anyway?

LYN    Orlando – it's in central Florida.

ANN    Sounds OK – are you going on your own?

LYN    Yes, but I don't mind that. There'll be other people on the tour and I'm sure to make friends. You know I like meeting new people. Here, let me show you the brochure.

ANN    It looks pretty packed – will you really have time to do all these things?

LYN    Oh, yes, it's all planned. Let's see – Day One we arrive in Orlando and after we've settled into our hotel, we have the afternoon free – I guess we can have a look around, or do what we like. Then Day Two we go to Disney World!

ANN    You mean Mickey Mouse and all that?

LYN    Yes, it's a kind of gigantic funfair with all the Walt Disney characters and there's also the Epcot Center – a sort of city of the future with all the latest developments. I've always wanted to go there ever since I saw it on television. And then on Day Three we go to Sea World.

ANN    Whatever's that?

LYN    Well, they have aquatic displays and pearl diving and performing dolphins and even a killer whale!

ANN    Can't say I like the sound of a killer whale much! Let's see what you do on Day Four. Oh, it seems to be free.

LYN    Yes, that's right and then on the next day we go to the Kennedy Space Center. That should be interesting.

ANN    I wonder how much they let you see – that's where NASA is, isn't it?

LYN    Well, I shouldn't think you'd be able to see the latest spacecraft, but you might be allowed a glimpse of Mission Control and perhaps watch how they receive messages from satellites. Anyway, I bet you learn a lot more about space than you ever knew before.

ANN    Mmm – I quite envy you going there. Somehow, I find it quite hard to believe that people will one day live out in space.

LYN    Oh, I don't. I'd give it a try if I had the chance. Now, what next? Oh yes, Day Six – Circus World.

ANN    Circus World. That sounds fun. I love going to the circus.

LYN    So do I. It says here: Circus World – see – take part – enjoy. I wonder what 'take part' involves!

ANN    You'll soon find out!

LYN    And then Day Seven, we come home. Just as well, I'll be broke by then.

ANN    I suppose you've been saving up for ages for this holiday.

LYN    Well, I *was*, but then I bought some new clothes, you know what it's like. I did think of putting in some extra hours at work, but the money wasn't really worth it after tax and it would've meant I didn't get home till late. Dad offered to lend me some money, but I know he really needs it himself. In the end I went to see my bank manager. He was terribly nice – so here I am all booked up and ready to go.

## FOURTH PART

*In the fourth part of the test you will hear a director explaining scenery positions and rehearsing stage moves with the actors. Look at the diagrams on Pages 56–8 and for questions 20 and 21 tick one of the boxes A, B, C or D. For question 22 write the names of the different acts and scenes in the boxes beside the diagrams. You will hear the piece twice.*

Good morning everybody. As you know, in this opera you are required to move certain pieces of the scenery as well as act, in this way the action is not held up. So if you would like to look at your diagram you will see Act 1, Scene 1 ready set as it will appear at the start of the opera. The four pieces of scenery have been marked A, B, C and D and your positions on stage shown in relation to them. Stage right and stage left have been marked as seen from your positions on stage when you're facing the audience.

Now what I would like to do this morning is rehearse the moves between scenes, so if you would like to take up your positions, we'll begin. To move from Act 1, Scene 1 to Act 1, Scene 2, first move piece A to stage right, slightly downstage and with the long side of the scenery pointing diagonally to centre stage. Next, move piece B to a similar position but at stage left. Move piece C upstage to butt onto piece D. Right, let's go through that again. A to stage right and B to stage left and piece C upstage to meet D. Good. . .

Now, let's walk through Act 2, Scene 1 – it's rather tricky so listen carefully. What we're aiming to do is form a triangle without a base, so will A and B move upstage centre and swing round to form a triangle, the apex pointing upstage, while C and D move downstage as far as the curtain and line up the long sides of the scenery to form a continuation of the AB triangle. C should now be downstage right and D downstage left. This gives us the two sides of the triangle as AC and BD. To move to positions for Act 2, Scene 2, A and B move to centre stage but keep your triangle formation. C and D swing round and form an inverse triangle downstage centre and backing onto AB. OK, back to Act 2, Scene 1 positions and let's do that change again. A and B keep your triangle formation but move slightly downstage centre. C and D swing round, form your inverse triangle and butt onto A and B. Fine.

The change from Act 2, Scene 2 to Act 2, Scene 3 is very fast and requires concentration – so here goes. A and B move upstage and reverse your triangle position so the apex is now pointing downstage. C move downstage right as far as the curtain line and position scenery so that the long side is pointing diagonally to centre stage. D do the same stage left. Good, no problems there. Now for the last scene, Act 2, Scene 4. C and D hold your positions. A move downstage right, swing your piece of scenery to form a triangle with C, the apex pointing centre stage. B do the same stage left, swing round and form a triangle with D, the apex pointing stage centre. Good. Now let's take it from the top and walk through the complete scene changes in the opera.


## TEST FOUR: KEY

### PAPER 1

Section A

| | | | | | |
|---|---|---|---|---|---|
| 1 | D | 10 | A | 18 | A |
| 2 | C | 11 | C | 19 | B |
| 3 | C | 12 | D | 20 | D |
| 4 | A | 13 | B | 21 | D |
| 5 | C | 14 | C | 22 | A |
| 6 | B | 15 | B | 23 | C |
| 7 | B | 16 | A | 24 | D |
| 8 | C | 17 | C | 25 | D |
| 9 | D | | | | |

Section B

| *First Passage* | *Second Passage* | *Third Passage* |
|---|---|---|
| 26  B | 31  C | 35  B |
| 27  C | 32  D | 36  D |
| 28  D | 33  B | 37  A |
| 29  C | 34  C | 38  C |
| 30  A | | 39  C |
| | | 40  A |

## PAPER 3

### Section A

**1**

| | |
|---|---|
| 1  aware/conscious | 11  associated/linked |
| 2  quality/scope | 12  how/what |
| 3  such | 13  often/frequently/sometimes |
| 4  development/growth | 14  much/far |
| 5  based | 15  indicated/suggested/showed |
| 6  proof/evidence | 16  reflect/show/match/fit/follow |
| 7  make | 17  problems/things |
| 8  as/that/which | 18  personal/own/various |
| 9  other | 19  strong |
| 10  At | 20  reaction/response |

**2**  a)  Although the weather was bad/it was bad weather, everyone enjoyed the fair.

b)  She plays chess more imaginatively/with more imagination than her sister.

c)  The supervisor instructed the men not to touch the rocker switch.

d)  The importance of a good family life should never be underestimated.

e)  It was such a hard punch that it broke the boxer's nose.

f)  Hardly had I closed the door when a shot rang out.

g)  Beer is made/brewed from hops and malt.

h)  It is not so much the writing of articles I dislike, but typing them.

**3**  a)  had better/should/ought to take an

b)  I had known

c)  didn't know/couldn't remember

d)  go to the cinema/football match, etc.

e)  don't you do/not do

f)  still couldn't/wasn't able to make her

**4**  a)  Despite his old age/being very old, he still walks round the park every day.

b)  I didn't know you came from Brazil.

c)  Although he's a brilliant scientist, he's also rather stupid.

d)  I'd never seen her/have thought she could eat so much.

e)  In the end he gave in to pressure from the others.

f)  Have you (got) any proof of your allegations?

g)  Simon could hardly read or write.

h)  Her motives were incomprehensible to him.

## Section B

5   *Candidates' answers to these questions may vary considerably in structure, expression and interpretation of the passage. Candidates should, however, be able to demonstrate comprehension of the gist of the passage and the writer's intentions and an understanding of particular words or phrases. The following are suggested answers:*

a)   A book.

b)   Hatred of something.

c)   That books could be bright, interesting and imaginative but they became heavy, dull and boring when they were text books.

d)   Dullness.

e)   Textbooks.

f)   Imitations of valuable, precious or desirable ideas.

g)   The pupils/readers of the textbook.

h)   That they became mundane and unexciting lists.

i)   Obscure writing that is difficult to understand.

j)   He implies that the ploy of using uninteresting texts was to prevent the student from having original thought or happiness.

k)   The hard work necessary when using this type of textbook.

l)   As he grew older he became more discriminating.

m)   *Main points*: Textbooks as the most boring of books; often obligatory reading and dull; interesting facts presented without excitement; belief that learning from these was good for the spirit; worst example of all *The Invertebrata*; complex language with no sentiment.

## PAPER 4

| First Part | | Second Part | | Third Part | | Fourth Part | |
|---|---|---|---|---|---|---|---|
| 1 | City Radio | 8 | False | 16 | B | 20 | B |
| 2 | Four million | 9 | True | 17 | B | 21 | D |
| 3 | The radio station's | 10 | True | 18 | A | 22 | C |
| | tenth birthday. | 11 | False | 19 | C | | |
| 4 | Sunday 18th October | 12 | False | | | | |
| 5 | Battersea Park | 13 | True | | | | |
| 6 | 50 | 14 | False | | | | |
| 7 | Fig. 1 Woodmice | 15 | True | | | | |
| | Fig. 2 Woodpecker | | | | | | |
| | Fig. 3 Squirrel | | | | | | |
| | Fig. 4 Blue tit | | | | | | |

## TEST FOUR: TAPESCRIPT

## FIRST PART

*For the first part of the test you will hear part of a radio programme. Look at Page 75 in your test book. For questions 1–6 fill in correct answers. For question 7 write the answer in the boxes. You will hear the conversation twice.*

Good afternoon everybody. Well, here at City Radio we've set up the biggest acorn hunt in history. In association with the Wildlife Trust and Friends of the Earth, we are organising a mammoth acorn hunt in October. And we want you, our 4 million listeners, to search London for acorns to plant to commemorate our 10th Birthday. We are arranging for special acorn hunts to take place in five London parks , starting at ten in the morning on Sunday 18th October. We will be concentrating our efforts at Battersea Park where the City cruiser will be in the centre of the park to act as a base. Any child celebrating a tenth birthday on that day will be especially welcome; and listen you birthday kids, the first 50 of you to arrive at the cruiser will receive a special commemorative T-shirt and a bag of City 'goodies' — so get out there early.

Remember though, it isn't just a question of picking up the odd acorn to plant for yourself, the idea is to collect hundreds of acorns for the Wildlife Trust to grow as well. We hope to make this the biggest acorn hunt ever, so that the London of the future will abound in oak trees.

The more acorns that are sown, the more we will be doing to encourage urban wildlife and that is why we have concentrated on the oak tree – it supports the richest mixture of animal life. Did you know over 300 species of insect can live in the oak, some of them forming important food sources for birds? Acorns provide food for small animals such as mice, rats and squirrels as well, while the trees offer shelter and nesting places. Be careful though, before planting your acorns make sure that they are in good condition and haven't been nibbled or pecked by animals or birds. If you do find a damaged acorn you might like to identify what's been attacking it, so here's what to look for:

If the acorn is just nibbled at one end then probably woodmice are the culprits. Whereas if a hole has been neatly pecked in one side, near the top of the acorn, then that is the work of a small bird – the blue tit. Squirrels crack open the acorns before they start eating them, while the woodpecker sits in the tree and pecks out the centre of the acorn before abandoning the outer case. So, do a bit of detective work while you're collecting.

So, that's it, get out there collecting and remember 'Great oaks from little acorns grow'. See you at Battersea on October 18th for the biggest acorn hunt in history.

## SECOND PART

*Listen carefully to the conversation which follows. For each of the questions 8–15 on Page 76 tick whether the statement is true or false. You will hear the conversation twice.*

| RICHARD | Hello, Hilary. Haven't seen you for a long time. What are you doing now? |
|---|---|
| HILARY | Oh, hello Richard. Well, I've still got my dance company and I teach dance at North London Poly and in the City, but, here's the exciting bit, I've also got another job as well. |
| RICHARD | My God, I don't know how you do it. Well, go on then, tell me all about it. |
| HILARY | Well, don't laugh but I'm a singing telegram girl. |
| RICHARD | A what? You mean you go around singing and delivering telegrams? |
| HILARY | Well, yes, we dress up in different costumes – in fact we do practically everything – including gorillas. |
| RICHARD | Gorillas! I can't imagine that being very popular. |
| HILARY | Well, there you're wrong! It's one of the most asked for and I like being a gorilla. I go absolutely berserk, zooming about, jumping on people and throwing peanuts at them. And a lot of people want tap-dancing gorillas so my dance training comes in handy. |
| RICHARD | Sound dreadful! What other ghastly things do you have to do? |
| HILARY | Let's see – yes, one of my favourites is being a French maid where I put on an accent and go around tickling people with my feather duster. |
| RICHARD | I'm amazed you don't get arrested! |
| HILARY | Don't be silly, people love it. You do have to judge your audience though, especially if you're going to be boisterous. If there are children I don't want to frighten them and the last thing we ever want to do is offend anyone. |
| RICHARD | The whole idea of barging in on someone and embarrassing them by performing all over their home or office I think is pretty offensive. |
| HILARY | Oh you're just stuffy and old-fashioned, Richard. More and more people are asking for our services and their requests are getting more and more bizarre. |
| RICHARD | Go on then, tell me the worst. |
| HILARY | Well I suppose the most ridiculous thing I've done is be a tap-dancing Christmas pudding. |
| RICHARD | Oh no! However did you get into this job? |
| HILARY | It all started when a college friend of mine got a loan from her bank manager by singing her request to him! With the money she started Send a Song, the first company in London to do singing |

telegrams. I used to help her out at first but, because I'm a dancer and there are quite a lot of requests for tap-dancing, I now do about four jobs a week.

RICHARD    Well, I hope the money's good.

HILARY    Um, not bad. I get somewhere between £10 and £20 a job and it only lasts five minutes.

RICHARD    You mean people actually pay £20 to be embarrassed!

HILARY    No, of course not. They send the telegrams to their friends and colleagues.

RICHARD    Hm, more like enemies! Still I suppose it's pretty easy money for you.

HILARY    The worst part is getting to the places, it can be a bit chaotic especially if I'm doing more than one telegram in an evening. Sometimes you can wear the costumes underneath each other – a Wonderwoman outfit under your gorilla suit, for instance – but it's not always possible so you have to find somewhere to change. I've become rather good at changing in my car.

RICHARD    That must raise some comments from passers-by.

HILARY    No, curiously enough, most people just don't notice and in the City of London I can walk around as a gorilla and none of the City gents pays me any attention at all. The cabbies are great though, they'll hoot and even stop the traffic.

RICHARD    Does anyone ever object to their telegram?

HILARY    Oh no. We go to lot of trouble to find out as much about them as possible then we can write a really personal song, including all their little habits, hobbies, secrets and family jokes. Quite often we don't understand them, but they always get a laugh. After all, we're entertainers! We don't mind making people blush, but we don't want to make them cringe!


## THIRD PART

*For the third part you will hear a conversation about a local swimming pool. For questions 16–19 on Pages 76–7, you should tick one of the boxes A, B, C or D. You will hear the conversation twice.*

WOMAN    Excuse me, sir. Would you like to sign this petition?

MAN    Petition? What for?

WOMAN    Well, I expect you know the council are proposing to close our local swimming pool.

MAN    Oh, that won't bother me. I never go swimming except in the sea.

WOMAN    But it's the children we're worried about. You see they'll have to go to Amsford if they close the pool – and that's four miles away. I mean, someone will have to take them and fetch them if they're young, and then there's the problem of the buses. It'll be a terrible shame if our Bonfield children have to go all that way for a swim.

MAN    I'm afraid I'm not all that worried about children. I haven't got any.

WOMAN    Oh, I see. But I'm sure you'll agree all children ought to learn to swim. You hear of terrible accidents at the seaside . . . children drowning . . .

MAN    It's up to the parents to keep them under control, if you ask me. They shouldn't let the kids in the water if they can't swim.

WOMAN    But that's just the point – they've got to learn somewhere. And it isn't only the children. There are lots of adults in Bonfield who enjoy swimming – keep-fit enthusiasts, sportsmen and women, to say nothing of some of the old people who find a gentle swim does wonders for their rheumatism. It may be out of the question for them to get to Amsford more than once in a while. So, if you wouldn't mind signing, you'd really be doing something for the people of Bonfield and yourself too, of course.

MAN    Bonfield? I don't think Bonfield's problems are anything to do with me. I don't happen to live in this area.


## FOURTH PART

*Listen to the following conversation and look at questions 20–22 on Page 77 in your test book. For each question put a tick in one of the boxes A, B, C or D. You will hear the conversation twice.*

MAN    Excuse me, can I ask you – what do you give your children for breakfast?

WOMAN    Well, they usually have an egg, or a bit of toast. They don't always finish it if they're late though.

MAN     Have you tried giving them Glo-flakes?

WOMAN   Glo-flakes? What's that? Another breakfast cereal?

MAN     Not just another breakfast cereal. It's the breakfast food that keeps you warm inside – all the time – no matter how bleak the weather is. Children love it and they get a Glo sticker in every packet. Also, if they collect ten tokens from the boxes they can become a Glo Club member and get a badge and a magazine. Every child should have a chance to become a Glo child.

WOMAN   Well, I wouldn't mind trying it. They've got quite a walk to the bus stop and it gets very cold on winter mornings.

MAN     Your worries are over. Give them Glo-flakes and they'll be warm inside and out.

# TEST FIVE: KEY

## PAPER 1

Section A

| | | | | | |
|---|---|---|---|---|---|
| 1 | B | 10 | C | 18 | D |
| 2 | A | 11 | C | 19 | A |
| 3 | B | 12 | A | 20 | B |
| 4 | A | 13 | C | 21 | A |
| 5 | C | 14 | B | 22 | C |
| 6 | A | 15 | D | 23 | D |
| 7 | B | 16 | B | 24 | D |
| 8 | D | 17 | B | 25 | B |
| 9 | B | | | | |

### Section B

| First Passage | | Second Passage | | Third Passage | |
|---|---|---|---|---|---|
| 26 | A | 31 | B | 36 | A |
| 27 | D | 32 | B | 37 | C |
| 28 | C | 33 | A | 38 | C |
| 29 | C | 34 | C | 39 | A |
| 30 | C | 35 | D | 40 | B |

## PAPER 3

Section A

| 1 | 1 | one | 8 | version/representation | 15 | this/such |
|---|---|---|---|---|---|---|
| | 2 | across | 9 | You/But | 16 | quite/somewhat/rather/much |
| | 3 | exhibit | 10 | complete | 17 | pair |
| | 4 | shape | 11 | Once | 18 | lift/open |
| | 5 | designed/made | 12 | glow/shine | 19 | reveals/becomes/is |
| | 6 | rested/hung/was | 13 | on | 20 | was/is |
| | 7 | what/how | 14 | time | | |

2  a)   The son was told/warned by his mother never to do it again.

     b)   There's no point in telling her anything.

     c)   It's time I painted my garage./had my garage painted./my garage was painted.

     d)   'You can't enter the bank', said the security guard.

     e)   Your car shouldn't be parked there, it is against the law.

f) A woman with advertising experience was what the director was looking for.

g) I stopped smoking ten years ago.

h) Nobody has bought that Fiat yet.

3  a) although she knew
   b) he would be quiet
   c) it's cheaper/more convenient
   d) have to go/go
   e) I didn't keep you waiting/you haven't been waiting
   f) have them done

4  a) On no account may/must you/are you to leave early.
   b) When I was a child I used to be a hopscotch champion.
   c) I don't care for her choice of friends.
   d) He had a mind of his own./He made up his mind to have his own way.
   e) Whatever happens, you mustn't lose the money./Whatever you do, don't lose the money.
   f) He never listens to my requests.
   g) I must say he gets on with the job/his work.
   h) There was no sign of trouble at the demonstration.

## Section B

5  *Candidates' answers to these questions may vary considerably in structure, expression and interpretation of the passage. Candidates should, however, be able to demonstrate comprehension of the gist of the passage and the writer's intentions and an understanding of particular words or phrases. The following are suggested answers:*

   a) Because it is very tempting to ignore reality and have fantasies about the future.
   b) It means to pleasantly spend time that otherwise would be boring.
   c) fascinating, seductive, absorbing.
   d) Reality is being tamed. This means that you can adapt reality to fit in with your dreams.
   e) The 'euphoria' that you can reach in your fantasies.
   f) Future reality.
   g) A daydream that is not checked by reality.
   h) The 'new science' is futurology – the forecasting of the future.
   i) 'literally parochial' means geographically local and mundane.
   j) The unpleasant predictions.
   k) Because people will not change their daily lives as a consequence of the prediction.
   l) The certainties of the long-term future and its inevitable catastrophies.
   m) The species will probably become extinct but a new life form will evolve.
   n) *Main points*: people fascinated by future; enjoyment of planning; fantasy can take over; futurologists' careers depend on this and make far-reaching or parochial, long-term or short term predictions; people more interested in the next 10–25 years as they won't experience the effects of the long-term.

## PAPER 4

| First Part | Second Part | Third Part |
|---|---|---|
| 1  i | 7  False | 17  B |
|    ii | 8  True | 18  C |
|    iii | 9  False | 19  A |
| 2  i, iv, v | 10  False | |
| 3  B | 11  False | |
| 4  B | 12  True | |
| 5  C | 13  False | |
| 6  C | 14  False | |
|  | 15  True | |
|  | 16  False | |

# TEST FIVE: TAPESCRIPT

## FIRST PART

*For the first part of the test you will hear a lecture about back pain. Look at Pages 96–7 of your test book. Read the questions and instructions carefully. You will hear the piece twice.*

Good morning, ladies and gentlemen. As you know, this morning's lecture is about back pain, one of the most common medical ailments in the developed countries today. For example, in Great Britain, the Back Pain Association tells us that 89,000 people are off work every day due to back pain; that is some 20 million working days are lost per annum. But can we believe these statistics? I fear not, because the Back Pain Association interprets the word 'work' as 'those people who are employed'. Clearly, this does not take into account the vast army of mothers, housewives, children and students who are not officially 'working'. As a recent father myself, I can vouch for the fact that a mother works twice as hard as the average employee, and she does not get adequately paid for it. As a doctor with a busy practice, I am not able to give my wife all the help that I would like to, therefore she copes with our baby alone most of the day. As there are many women, and some men, in the same position with babies, or young children, and no help, I should like to concentrate on their back pain problems today.

There are a number of factors which can eventually lead up to a severe bout of back pain. When the child is young a lot of time is spent in lifting it up and putting it down. All too often this is done in a hurried way and proper lifting techniques are not employed – resulting in a weakening of joints, ligaments and muscles which ultimately can produce back pain. Much cot-making is necessary at this stage, washing baby clothes, changing baby and a whole host of other back-bending acts. If the mother is overweight, has previous back problems or is not receiving adequate nutrition, then back pain may strike her down. It may be insidious in onset but it slowly and surely progresses to a full blown attack of sciatica. Even today in the 1980s, with our luxury kitchens containing a vast array of labour-saving devices, people still stand badly, hoover badly, iron badly, walk badly and even sleep badly!

So what can be done to prevent back pain occurring in this very important section of society? Well, firstly, women must ensure that their diet is adequate in nutrition. A diet may well be filling but if the food consists mainly of packaged or tinned goods then it could lead to undernourishment. All processed foods have been treated with a host of chemicals such as preservatives, emulsifiers, anti-staling agents, anti-oxidants, colourings, etc. Very often the manufacturers nobly claim that they have added extra vitamins and sometimes minerals to their products, but this claim is a joke because if the food had not been processed in the first place then there would be no need to reconstitute it with synthetic vitamins or minerals, the natural ones having been 'laundered' out in the processing. There is an enormous body of evidence to show that denutrified food robs us of adequate nutrition and can weaken ligaments, muscles and tendons and so opening up the possibility of back pain developing.

Secondly, women should pay attention to their posture and movement. A mother's posture is of crucial importance whilst she is caring for a baby or young child. What often seems natural may often result in disaster. For example, holding or carrying the baby on her hip. This requires the mother to side-bend her spine away from the baby to allow the child to be adequately supported by the illiac crest, which is to say the sticking-out part of the pelvis. When someone bends in this way, it puts pressure on the nerve roots in the spine at the side to which she is bending and stretches the spinal ligaments and muscles at the side on which the baby is supported. Consequently, this stretching can produce inflammation which in turn produces swelling which in turn puts pressure on the nerves in the area and can produce back pain. This process repeated often enough over a longish period of time will almost certainly produce disastrous results. It has often been said, but it is worth repeating, that bending forward at the waist should be avoided and that picking up should always take place by keeping the upper body straight and bending at the knees. This is a difficult technique to master at first, and people often forget it, but to avoid back pain developing, it should be practised until it comes naturally.

Making beds, standing at sinks for a long time, picking up baby, bathing baby, changing baby, hoovering, cooking and other household activities which require bending are dangerous if executed wrongly. Worktops should be high enough to negate the need to bend forward whilst carrying out work functions. Cleaning the bath and making the beds should be done in a kneeling position; happily, many people now use duvets and bed-making is not as dangerous as it used to be. Standing for long periods of time should be avoided and lifting babies should be done in the way previously described.

So, to sum up, mothers, or indeed anyone involved in looking after babies or children or carrying out household tasks, should pay particular care to their posture and moving techniques and ensure that they have a good, nutritious diet. In this way they should be able to avoid the plague of back pain.


## SECOND PART

*In the second part you will hear part of an interview on a radio programme. Look at Page 97 in your test book and read the statements carefully. Tick whether they are true or false. You will hear the interview twice.*

| | |
|---|---|
| INTERVIEWER | This afternoon we have in the studio Tony Jones, who was a 'townie' until he got the call of the countryside and went to live there five years ago. Tony, who experienced all of the pitfalls of country living in the beginning, is here to offer advice to any of you who hanker after a rural retreat. Right then, Tony what made you take off to the country in the first place? |
| TONY | Well, I suppose anyone who moves to the country wants their life to be different in some way. I mean, if you have always lived in a city, as I had, then something must happen to make you want to move . . . in my case I was made redundant and, when it came to looking around for a new job, I just couldn't face going back into an office again. So I sat down and thought about what I'd really like to do. |
| INTERVIEWER | And that, I suppose, turned out to be something in the country? |
| TONY | No, initially I didn't think of moving, but just of getting a different kind of job, you know social work with kids or old people, that kind of thing. |
| INTERVIEWER | So, what happened, why didn't you? |
| TONY | Well, I hadn't got any of the right qualifications, and it would have taken me two years to have qualified . . . and I certainly didn't want to go back to formal education again. |
| INTERVIEWER | Couldn't you have learned while on the job . . . sort of picked it up as you went along? |
| TONY | No, you have to have a diploma. Anyway, after talking it over with friends who had moved out I thought I'd like to give it a try – after all, a change of scene . . . |
| INTERVIEWER | Is better than . . . yes, we all know that. So, where did you go when you did decide to move? |
| TONY | I went right out – to Shropshire. After all I thought if you're going to go rural you might as well do it properly. The first problem though was how was I going to make a living – there are fewer jobs in the country, so I decided to start up on my own. |
| INTERVIEWER | That's pretty ambitious, a townie moving off to the depths of the country *and* setting up his own business. How did you start, had you got any skills? |
| TONY | I'd always had a garden and grown some vegetables and flowers, you know, usual things, salad stuff, carrots, peas, beans, a bit of fruit, some roses . . . so I thought of a smallholding, a kind of small farm. But when I looked at the prices to buy, I changed my mind; I didn't have that kind of money. |
| INTERVIEWER | OK a farm's out – so what next? |
| TONY | I settled on a nursery and bought my way into a partnership with a bloke who had just started up. There was a cottage on the land where we were going to have the nursery, so the accommodation problem was solved as well. Mind you, the number of things that needed doing to that cottage . . . but anyway, we got started, put our greenhouses up, planted our flowers and fruit and waited. |
| INTERVIEWER | You mean you waited for the stuff to grow? |
| TONY | No, we waited for the customers to come! We had forgotten the first rule of starting your own business: publicity. Nobody knew we were there! |
| INTERVIEWER | How did you get round that? |
| TONY | Well, we put some adverts in the local press, had some brochures printed and distributed them, put up some posters in the nearby villages, but I think the big breakthrough came when we got on local radio. |
| INTERVIEWER | Ah, the power of the airwaves! That got the customers rolling in, did it? |

| | |
|---|---|
| TONY | Yes, I must say, things started to look up and now we've become quite famous and have a gardening spot on local TV. |
| INTERVIEWER | Good for you. But, tell me, Tony, was it all worth it? |
| TONY | Oh yes, I wouldn't come back to town for anything now, but it was certainly hard work in the beginning . . . we worked from dawn to dusk, sixteen, eighteen hours a day sometimes. And the things that went wrong . . the drainage system, heating in the greenhouses failing, a winter with three months of rain, the wind blowing over young trees, the roof of the cottage collapsing . . . I could go on for ever. |
| INTERVIEWER | Sounds alarming. Now, one last thing before you shoot back to your plants, Tony. What advice would you give anyone contemplating following in your footsteps? |
| TONY | Well, the one thing I would say is persevere . . . if you really want to make country living work, you must find something you enjoy doing and here you can make use of any skills or hobbies you already have, and then it is just hard work . . . oh, and yes, most important of all, a sense of humour. |
| INTERVIEWER | That's pretty good advice. Thanks again, Tony, for coming in and good luck with the nursery. Now, anyone who would like to write in to me . . . |

## THIRD PART

*Listen to the following announcement. Tick one of the boxes A, B, C or D on Page 98 in your test book. You will hear the piece twice.*

Good afternoon, ladies and gentlemen. Welcome to Selfridges. In our leisure department on the first floor, we have a free demonstration today of the new Sunshine Sunbed – safe, soft and fully mobile. No electricity needed – it runs on its own batteries so you can switch on anywhere, in the garden, on your balcony, in the bedroom or even in the kitchen while the dinner's cooking. And, that's not all, with every sunbed we're giving away a pair of sunglasses and a bottle of suntan lotion. Come and try it for yourself now – no obligation to purchase. Melanie from Sunshine Beds is waiting to help you. Come and start soaking up the sun before you go on that beach holiday. You'll be amazed at the result. Five minutes sheer bliss and a glass of tropical fruit juice with our compliments. Hurry now – don't miss this opportunity. And don't forget if you want to buy, we can arrange easy terms with no interest charges.